CAMBRIDGE LIBRARY COLLECTION

Books of enduring scholarly value

Archaeology

The discovery of material remains from the recent or the ancient past has always been a source of fascination, but the development of archaeology as an academic discipline which interpreted such finds is relatively recent. It was the work of Winckelmann at Pompeii in the 1760s which first revealed the potential of systematic excavation to scholars and the wider public. Pioneering figures of the nineteenth century such as Schliemann, Layard and Petrie transformed archaeology from a search for ancient artifacts, by means as crude as using gunpowder to break into a tomb, to a science which drew from a wide range of disciplines - ancient languages and literature, geology, chemistry, social history - to increase our understanding of human life and society in the remote past.

The Mycenaean Tree and Pillar Cult and Its Mediterranean Relations

Sir Arthur John Evans (1851–1941), the pioneer of ancient Cretan archaeology, most famously excavated the ruins of Knossos and uncovered the remains of its Bronze Age Minoan civilisation (as detailed in *The Palace of Minos at Knossos*, also reissued in this series). In this highly illustrated work, first published in 1901, Evans surveys the recent archaeological evidence from his dig at Knossos as well as from other locations around the Mediterranean. He describes a variety of religious objects and symbols, especially those concerned with sacred stones, pillars and trees, which Evans argues are characteristic of religious worship in the Mycenaean period. He considers in particular the importance of the Cretan double-axe symbol, the labrys, its close link with depictions of bulls and its association with the labyrinth of Knossos. Elsewhere he examines the symbolism of the Lion Gate at Mycenae and finds parallels with similar artefacts found in Crete and Egypt.

Cambridge University Press has long been a pioneer in the reissuing of out-of-print titles from its own backlist, producing digital reprints of books that are still sought after by scholars and students but could not be reprinted economically using traditional technology. The Cambridge Library Collection extends this activity to a wider range of books which are still of importance to researchers and professionals, either for the source material they contain, or as landmarks in the history of their academic discipline.

Drawing from the world-renowned collections in the Cambridge University Library and other partner libraries, and guided by the advice of experts in each subject area, Cambridge University Press is using state-of-the-art scanning machines in its own Printing House to capture the content of each book selected for inclusion. The files are processed to give a consistently clear, crisp image, and the books finished to the high quality standard for which the Press is recognised around the world. The latest print-on-demand technology ensures that the books will remain available indefinitely, and that orders for single or multiple copies can quickly be supplied.

The Cambridge Library Collection brings back to life books of enduring scholarly value (including out-of-copyright works originally issued by other publishers) across a wide range of disciplines in the humanities and social sciences and in science and technology.

The Mycenaean Tree
and Pillar Cult and Its
Mediterranean Relations

With Illustrations from Recent Cretan Finds

ARTHUR JOHN EVANS

CAMBRIDGE
UNIVERSITY PRESS

CAMBRIDGE UNIVERSITY PRESS

Cambridge, New York, Melbourne, Madrid, Cape Town,
Singapore, São Paolo, Delhi, Mexico City

Published in the United States of America by Cambridge University Press, New York

www.cambridge.org
Information on this title: www.cambridge.org/9781108060912

© in this compilation Cambridge University Press 2013

This edition first published 1901
This digitally printed version 2013

ISBN 978-1-108-06091-2 Paperback

THE

MYCENAEAN TREE AND PILLAR CULT

AND ITS MEDITERRANEAN RELATIONS

THE

MYCENAEAN TREE AND PILLAR CULT

AND

ITS MEDITERRANEAN RELATIONS

WITH ILLUSTRATIONS FROM RECENT CRETAN FINDS

BY

ARTHUR J. EVANS, M.A., F.S.A.

KEEPER OF THE ASHMOLEAN MUSEUM
AND HON. FELLOW OF BRASENOSE COLLEGE, OXFORD

WITH A COLOURED PLATE AND SEVENTY FIGURES IN THE TEXT

London

MACMILLAN AND CO., Limited

NEW YORK: THE MACMILLAN COMPANY

1901

Richard Clay and Sons, Limited,
London and Bungay

PREFATORY NOTE

THIS work is reproduced by permission from the *Journal of Hellenic Studies*. It was communicated in its present form to the Hellenic Society in November, 1900, but the views here expressed regarding the character of Mycenaean worship and such external features as the baetylic pillars within the shrines and the 'horns of consecration' were, in their main outlines, first put forth by me in a paper on '*Pillar and Tree Worship in Mycenaean Greece*,' read in the Anthropological Section of the British Association at Liverpool in 1896. A short abstract of this was published in the Annual Report of the Association. In November, 1899, the part specially affecting Dr. Reichel's theory of the '*Thronkultus*' was read to the Oxford Philological Society.

It had been my original intention to incorporate the present study in a work, in course of preparation by me, on the Mycenaean gems and signets, but the fresh evidence supplied by the Cretan discoveries has induced me to put it forth in a separate form. This seemed the more desirable, since the most recently expressed views on the subject, as for instance those contained in Dr. H. von Fritze's essay, '*Die Mykenischen Goldringe und ihre Bedeutung für das Sacralwesen*' (*Strena Helbigiana*, 1900, p. 73 *seqq.*), though in certain respects supplying a welcome corrective to Dr. Reichel's system, still, as I venture to think, betray a very imperfect recognition of some of the most essential features of the cult. The Author moreover still maintains the now antiquated and wholly untenable position that the engraved Signet-Rings found at Mycenae and elsewhere are imported 'Phoenician' fabrics. So far, on the other hand, as my own views are confirmatory of those expressed by Dr. von Fritze in the paper above cited, by Dr. Wolters in his remarks on the Knossian fresco, and again by Dr. Furtwängler in his monumental work on Ancient Gems, they have at least the value of having been independently arrived at.

Great pains have been taken in this work to secure adequate reproductions of the Mycenaean gems and signets, which are here, in almost all cases, enlarged to three diameters. For this purpose magnified photographs of the casts were first made, which (checked at the same time by the casts) have formed the basis of drawings by Mr. F. Anderson and Mr. C. J. Praetorius. In the case of the more convex intaglios photographic reproductions by themselves yield imperfect representations of the designs, owing to the deep shadow which, with a single light, is thrown over a large part of the field. It is hoped however that, by the double process referred to, the greatest possible measure of clearness and accuracy may have been attained. A few drawings were executed by Monsieur E. Gilliéron at Athens, who also made the very careful copy of the Temple Fresco reproduced in the Plate by Mr. Griggs.

TABLE OF SECTIONS AND ILLUSTRATIONS

PAGE

§ 1.—Cretan Caves and Hypaethral Sanctuaries 1

    Fig. 1.—Gem from Vapheio Tomb, representing Daemons
    watering nurseling palms 3

§ 2.—Sacred Fig-Tree and Altar on a Pyxis from Knossos ... 3

    Fig. 2.—Fragment of Steatite Pyxis—Knossos 5

§ 3.—The Dove Cult of Primitive Greece 7

§ 4.—The Association of Sacred Tree and Pillar 7

§ 5.—The 'Labyrinth' and the Pillar Shrines of the God of
    the Double Axe 8

    Fig. 3.—Double Axe with Horns of Consecration between
    Bulls' Heads with similar Axes, on Mycenaean Vase from
    Old Salamis 9

    Fig. 4.—Gold Signet from Akropolis Treasure, Mycenae ($\frac{3}{1}$) ... 10

    Fig. 5.—Pillar of the Double Axes in Palace, Knossos 12

    Fig. 6.—Pillar Shrines and Votaries on Vase Fragment from
    Old Salamis, Cyprus 14

§ 6.—The Βαίτυλος and Baetylic Tables of Offering... 14

    Fig. 7.—Baetylic Table of Offering from the Diktaean Cave,
    restored 16

    Fig. 8.—Baetylic Cones and Offering Slabs on Hittite Seals ... 17

    Fig. 9.—Small Baetylic Altar from Cyrenaica... 17

    Fig. 10.—Baetylic Table used as a Base for Sacral Lions on
    Cretan Gem 18

    Fig. 11.—Baetylic Altar on Coin of Cretan Community... ... 18

PAGE

Fig. 12.—Impressed Glass Plaque from Mycenae, with Daemons
  pouring Libations on Sacred Cairn   19

Fig. 13.—Impressed Glass Plaque from Mycenae, with Daemons
  pouring Libations on Sacred Pillar   19

Fig. 14.—Impressed Glass Plaque from Mycenae, with Daemons
  pouring Libations on a Baetylic Tripod-Lebês   19

§ 7.—Zeus Kappôtes and the Meteoric Element in Baetylic
    Stones ...   .·...   20

§ 8.—Sepulchral Stelae as Baetylic Habitations of Departed
    Spirits   21

§ 9.—The Tomb of Zeus   21

§ 10.—Small Dimensions of the Mycenean Shrines   24

§ 11.—Aniconic Cult Images supplemented by Pictorial
    Representations of Divinities: Transitions to An-
    thropomorphism   25

Fig. 15.—Mycenaean Figurine of bronze from Cave of Hermês
  Kranaios, near Sybrita, Crete   27

Fig. 16.—Mycenaean Figurine of silver from Nezero, Thessaly...   28

§ 12.—Illustrative Survivals of Tree and Pillar Cult in
    Classical Greece and Italy   28

§ 13.—The Ficus Ruminalis   30

Fig. 17.—Infant and Horned Sheep from Clay Impression of
  Gem, Palace, Knossos ($\frac{3}{1}$)   31

§ 14.—Illustrative Value of Semitic Religious Sources   32

§ 15.—The Horns of Consecration   37

Fig. 18.—Horns of Consecration on Sanctuary Wall, from
  Fresco of Palace, Knossos...   38

Fig. 19.—Horned Cult Object of painted Pottery: Idaean
  Cave   38

Fig. 20.—Altar with Horned Cult Object above, from Stele of
  God Salm   39

Fig. 21.—Cone of Astarte within Horned Enclosure, Temple
  Court, Byblos. On Coin of Macrinus ($\frac{3}{1}$)...   40

PAGE

§ 16.—**Trinities and other Groups of Sacred Trees and Pillars** 40

Fig. 22.—Carthaginian Pillar Shrine on Stele, Nora, Sardinia... 41

Fig. 23.—Group of Sacred Pillars on Mycenaean Vase from Haliki 41

Fig. 24.—Worship of Group of Pillars on Cylinder, Mycenae (¾) 43

Fig. 25.—Worship of Group of Trees: Crystal Lentoid, Idaean Cave 44

Fig. 26.—Tree Trinity of God Min 45

§ 17.—**" The Pillar of the House "** 45

Fig. 27.—Sacred Column on Stele, Carthage 46

§ 18.—**Egyptian Influences and the Rayed Pillars of Mycenaean Cyprus** 48

Fig. 28.—Egyptian Palmette Pillars and the Rayed Pillars of Cyprus 51
  { Nos. 1–3.—Egyptian Pillars.
  { Nos. 4–7.—Cypro-Mycenaean derivatives.

Fig. 29.—Hathoric Uraeus Pillar and Cypro-Mycenaean and Oriental analogies 52
  { No. 1.—Egyptian Uraeus Pillar.
  { Nos. 2 and 3.—Cypro-Mycenaean Comparisons.
  { No. 4.—Dual Uraeus Staff of Istar.

§ 19.—**The Egyptian Element in the Animal Supporters of Mycenaean Trees and Columns** 54

§ 20.—**Sacred Trees and Foliated Pillars with Heraldically Posed Animals** 55

Fig. 30.—Sacred Tree and Wild Goats on Lentoid Gem, from Mycenae (¾) 56

Fig. 31.—Sacred Palm and Wild Goat on Lentoid Gem, Palaeokastro, Crete (¾) 56

Fig. 32.—Tree Pillar and Animals like Red Deer: Lentoid Gem, Goulàs, Crete (¾) 56

Fig. 33.—Fleur-de-lys Pillar and Confronted Sphinxes, on Gold Signet Ring, Mycenae (¾) 57

Fig. 34.—Pillar Tree with Young Bulls attached: on Crystal Signet Ring, Mycenae (¾) 58

PAGE

§ 21.—Architectural Columns with Animal Supporters : the Lions' Gate Type 58

 Fig. 35.—Tympanum Relief of Lions' Gate, Mycenae 59

 Fig. 36.—Pillar with Griffin Supporters : Lentoid Gem, Mycenae ($\frac{3}{1}$) 60

 Fig. 37.—Double-bodied Kriosphinx with Fore-feet on Base : Lentoid Gem, Mycenae ($\frac{2}{1}$) 61

 Fig. 38.—Double-bodied Lion with Fore-feet on Base : Lentoid Gem, Mycenae ($\frac{2}{1}$) 61

 Fig. 39.—Lions' Gate Type on Gold Signet Ring, Mycenae ($\frac{2}{1}$) 61

 Fig. 40.—Lions' Gate Type on Lentoid Gem, Zêro, Crete ($\frac{3}{1}$) ... 62

 Fig. 41.—Confronted Lions with Fore-feet on Baetylic Base : Lentoid Gem, Crete ($\frac{3}{1}$) 63

 Fig. 42 (*a* and *b*) Lion Supporters of Egyptian Solar Disk ... 64

§ 22.—Anthropomorphic Figures of Divinities substituted for the Baetylic Column in the Lions' Gate Scheme ... 65

 Fig. 43.—Male Divinity between Lions on Lentoid Gem, Kydonia, Crete ($\frac{3}{1}$) 65

 Fig. 44.—Female Divinity between Lions on Amygdaloid Gem, Mycenae ($\frac{3}{1}$) 66

 Fig. 45.—Seated Goddess between Lions on Lentoid Ring-Stone ($\frac{3}{1}$) 67

§ 23.—Mycenaean Daemons in Similar Heraldic Schemes ... 70

 Fig. 46.—Daemon between Two Lions on Lentoid Gem, Mycenae 70

§ 24.—A Mycenaean "Bethshemesh" 71

 Fig. 47.—Dual Pillar Worship on Cypro-Mycenaean Cylinder ($\frac{2}{1}$) 71

 Fig. 48.—Dual Pillar Worship on Gold Signet Ring from Knossos ($\frac{4}{1}$) 72

 Fig. 49.—Double Representation of Rayed Pillars on Tabloid Bead-Seal, Old Salamis 75

 Fig. 50.—Rayed Shield-bearing God on Painted Sarcophagus, Milato, Crete 76

§ 25.—Cult Scenes relating to a Warrior God and his Consort 77

 Fig. 51.—Armed God and Seated Goddess on Electrum Signet Ring, Mycenae 77

PAGE

Fig. 52.—Religious Scene on Gold Signet Ring from Vapheio Tomb ($\frac{3}{1}$) 78

Fig. 53.—Religious Scene on Gold Signet Ring from Mycenae ($\frac{3}{1}$) 79

Fig. 54.—Symbols derived from the Egyptian *Ankh*... 80
   1.—The Ankh.
   2.—Two-armed Egyptian Form (XVIIIth Dyn.).
   3 and 4.—Hittite Types.
   5.—From Mycenaean Ring (Fig. 52).
   6.—On Carthaginian Stele.

§ 26.—Sacred Gateways or Portal Shrines, mostly associated with Sacred Trees 83

Fig. 55.—Portal Shrine on Gold Signet Ring from Mycenae ($\frac{3}{1}$) 84

Fig. 56.—Cult Scene with Sacred Tree and Portal on Gold Signet Ring, Mycenae ($\frac{3}{1}$)... 84

Fig. 57.—Cult Scene with Sacred Tree and Portal, within *Temenos*, Mycenae ($\frac{3}{1}$) 85

Fig. 58.—Sacral Gateway and Votaries on Gold-plated Silver Ring, Mycenae ($\frac{3}{1}$) 86

Fig. 59.—Sacred Tree and Enclosure on Steatite Lentoid, Ligortino, Crete ($\frac{3}{1}$) 87

§ 27.—The Dolmen Shrines of Primitive Cult and the Dove Shrines of Mycenae 87

Fig. 60.—Baetylic Stone in Dolmen Shrine, Shiarai Hills, India 88

Fig. 61.—Pillared Chamber of 'Nau,' Minorca 89

Fig. 62 (*a* and *b*).—Plan and Section of 'Cova,' Minorca ... 90

Fig. 63.—Female Votaries before Pillar Shrine, Gold Signet Ring, Mycenae ($\frac{3}{1}$) 91

Fig. 64.—Goddess seated beside Pillar Shrine, on Gold Signet Ring, Mycenae ($\frac{3}{1}$). 92

Fig. 65.—Gold Shrine with Doves, Third Akropolis Grave, Mycenae (From Schliemann's 'Mycenae') 93

§ 28.—Fresco representing Small Baetylic Temple, from the Palace at Knossos 94

Fig. 66.—Façade of Small Mycenaean Temple, completed from the Fresco Painting of the Palace, Knossos. 95

PAGE

§ **29.—Parallels to the Baetylic Shrines of the Mycenaeans supplied by the Megalithic Sanctuaries of the Maltese Islands**   98

Fig. 67.—Pillar Cell of Hagiar Kim, Malta.   99

Fig. 68.—Spiral Ornament on Threshold of Baetylic Chapel, Giganteja, Gozo.   101

§ **30.—An Oriental Pillar Shrine in Macedonia and the Associated Worship**   102

Fig. 69.—Sacred Pillar in Shrine, Tekekiöi, Macedonia.   103

Fig. 70.—Plan of Shrine, Tekekiöi, Macedonia   104

COLOURED PLATE.

Façade of Small Mycenaean Temple from Fresco found in the Palace at Knossos ...   .

ERRATA.

P. 107, Note 1, *for* "ἀκόνκιον" *read* "ἀκόντιον."

P. [127], 12th line from bottom, *for* "object as its possession" *read* "object of its possession."

P. [140], 9th line from bottom, *for* "lentoid intaglio" *read* "cylinder."

P. [152], line 22, *for* "Ecbani" *read* "Heabani."

P. 156, bottom, *for* "archaelogical" *read* "archaeological."

P. 181, line 7, *for* "human divinity" *read* "departed human being."

THE

MYCENAEAN TREE AND PILLAR CULT
AND ITS MEDITERRANEAN RELATIONS

MYCENAEAN TREE AND PILLAR CULT AND ITS MEDITERRANEAN RELATIONS.

WITH ILLUSTRATIONS FROM RECENT CRETAN FINDS.

[PLATE V.]

§ 1.—*Cretan Caves and Hypaethral Sanctuaries.*

AMONG the greater monuments or actual structural remains of the Mycenaean world hitherto made known, it is remarkable how little there is to be found having a clear and obvious relation to religious belief. The great wealth of many of the tombs, the rich contents of the pit-graves of Mycenae itself, the rock-cut chambers, the massive vaults of the bee-hive tombs, are all indeed so many evidences of a highly developed cult of departed Spirits. The pit-altar over grave IV. of the Akropolis area at Mycenae, and the somewhat similar erection found in the Court-yard of the Palace at Tiryns, take us a step further in this direction; but it still remains possible that the second, like the first, may have been dedicated to the cult of the ancestors of the household, and it supplies in itself no conclusive evidences of a connexion with any higher form of worship. In the great South-Western Court, and again in the Central Area of the Palace of Knossos, have now, however, been brought to light the foundations of what seem to have been two rectangular altars; and the special relation in which this building stood to the God of the Double Axe makes a dedication to the Cretan Zeus in this case extremely probable.

In Crete indeed we are on somewhat different ground. Throughout the island are a series of caves, containing votive and sacrificial deposits, going back from the borders of the historic period to Mycenaean and still more remote antiquity. The two greatest of these, on the heights of Ida and Dikta, are connected by immemorial tradition with the cult of the ancient indigenous divinity later described by the Greeks as the Cretan Zeus, whose special symbol was the double axe. The colossal rock-hewn altar at the mouth of the Idaean Cave was unquestionably devoted to the service of this God.[1] In the steatite libation-table found at the bottom of the votive stratum of the Diktaean Cave[2] we have an article of cult the special

---

[1] F. Halbherr and P. Orsi, *Antro di Zeus Ideo*, p. 3 and Tav xi.

[2] *J.H.S.* xvii. (1897), p. 350 *seqq.*

significance of which will be pointed out in a succeeding section.[1] The thorough exploration of this cave, now carried out by Mr. D. G. Hogaith,[2] on behalf of the British School at Athens, has conclusively proved that the old traditions of the birth-place and oracular shrine of the Cretan Zeus attached themselves to this spot. The blasting away of the fallen rocks that encumbered the upper part of the grotto has in fact revealed a rude sacrificial altar and temenos covered with a votive deposit some seven feet deep, while the character of the divinity worshipped was sufficiently indicated by the large number of votive double axes found both here and in the inner sanctuary below. These double axes, as we shall see, may have actually embodied the presence of the God himself. His actual image in anthropomorphic shape was not needed by the religion of that time. The great mass of votive figures found in the sacrificial deposits of these Cretan caves bear no distinctive attributes of divinity. They seem, for the most part at least, to be simply miniature representations of human votaries and their domestic animals, who thus, according to a widespread practice, placed themselves and their belongings under the special protection of the higher powers.

It is possible, as I have elsewhere suggested,[3] that in a small building which occupies a most conspicuous position in the great prehistoric city of Goulas, in Crete, we have actually before us the remains of one of these Mycenaean shrines, originally containing a sacred tree. This is a small oblong building, about nine yards long by four wide, with walls originally breast high, consisting of two tiers of large roughly-squared blocks, the upper of which shows externally a projecting border, which recalls on a smaller scale the parapet of a great terrace wall that rises beyond it. The entrance to this low-walled enclosure on the small side to the north has mortised slabs on either side for the insertion of jambs, and must have consisted of a door-way higher than the walls themselves, and which may therefore have served some sacral purpose, the sanctity of the trilith or ritual doorway being widely prevalent in early religious cult, notably among the Phrygians.[4] Here, as in the case of a Knossian cult-scene, to be described below, the doorway of the enclosure may have had either in it or before it a sacred pillar, while the tree itself stood within the hypaethral shrine, spreading its boughs over its low walls and lintel. In front of this entrance is a large rock-cut cistern, originally no doubt, like other cisterns of Goulas, roofed in with the aid of limestone beams. In this connexion it may be noticed that the ritual watering of sacred trees, either from a natural or artificial source, is a regular feature of this form of worship. In the Mycenaean cult this is illustrated by the Vapheio

---

[1] See below, p. 15 *seqq.*

[2] See *Annual of the British School at Athens*, 1900.

[3] See my letter to the *Academy*, July 4, 1896, p. 18, and 'Goulas, the City of Zeus' (*Annual of the British School at Athens*, 1896). The recent French excavations on this site,

conducted by M. De Margne, have shown that a part of it at least was occupied by the inland Latô. But the fact remains incontestable that the overwhelming mass of existing remains belongs to the prehistoric period.

[4] See below, p. 83.

gem, representing two lion-headed daemons, who have filled two high-spouted vases from the basin of a fountain, and raise them above what appears to be a nurseling palm-tree [1] (Fig. 1). It may be noted that this religious cultivation of the young palms —then no doubt being largely introduced on to Greek soil by the cosmopolitan taste of the Mycenaean rulers—finds a later parallel in the Assyrian representations, first explained by Dr. Tylor, of winged genii fertilising the adult palm with the male cones. The parallelism is very suggestive.

FIG. 1.—GEM FROM VAPHEIO TOMB: DAEMONS WATERING NURSELING PALMS.

It is not necessary, indeed, to suppose that the sacred tree enclosed *ex hypothesi* in the Goulas shrine was a palm. A palm column, it is true, appears on a gem from this site [2] with two deer as supporters, in a scheme to be described below. But in Crete, as elsewhere in the Mycenaean world, there seems to have been a considerable variety of sacred trees. We recognise the pine and the cypress; and the abiding traditions of Knossos and Gortyna show how intimately the plane tree, which so often marks the presence of a spring, was bound up with the cult of the Cretan Zeus. The globular bunches of the tree, beneath which the Goddess sits on the signet from the Akropolis Treasure at Mycenae, have naturally suggested a vine. It will be seen from an interesting fragment from the site of Knossos that the fig must also be included among the sacred trees of the Mycenaeans.

§ 2.—*Sacred Fig-Tree and Altar on a Pyxis from Knossos.*

The object in question (Fig. 2) is a portion of a cylindrical vase or pyxis of dark steatite, decorated with reliefs, found on the slope of the hill known as *Gypsades*, which rises opposite to that on which the Palace of Knossos stands.[3] A remarkable feature of this fragment is that its lower margin is perforated by a rivet-hole, and shows other traces which indicate that the bottom of the cup was in a separate piece. The fact that at Palaeokastro, in Eastern Crete, an intaglio exhibiting dolphins and rocks in the same dark steatite, originally the bezel of a Mycenaean ring, was found covered with a thin plate of gold beaten into the design, suggests that in this case too the dull-coloured core may have been coated with the same brilliant material, and that the rivet holes may have partly served to attach the gold plate. It can be shown that the returning spiral designs of the oldest Mycenaean gold work are

---

[1] Apparently in a large pot : recalling the culture of nurseling palms at Bordighera, where they are largely cultivated for religious purposes, owing to a special privilege from the Pope.

[2] See p. 56, Fig. 32.

[3] It was obtained by me on the spot in 1894.

simply the translation into metal of the much more ancient steatite reliefs representing the same ornamentation. We may well believe that the steatite reliefs, like those of the fragment before us, gave birth in the same way to the figured designs in repoussé work, such as those that decorate the Vapheio vases, and that we here in fact see the intermediate stage of soft-stone carving, originally coated with a thin gold plate, which led up to more perfected art.

The design itself, so far as it is possible to study it in its fragmentary condition, presents so much naturalism and spirit that we may well believe that had the whole been preserved to us it would have afforded the nearest parallel to the marvellous gold cups from the Spartan tomb.

In the lowest zone of the composition, or, as we may call it, the foreground, appear parts of two male figures. The foremost of the two is in violent action, his right arm raised and his left thrown behind him. He is clad in the Mycenaean loin-clothing, and his feet were apparently swathed in the usual manner. Under his left shoulder fall long tresses of hair, recalling those that appear in the same position on the figures of the Vapheio cups and those of the Kefti tributaries on the tomb of Rekhmara. The prominent treatment of the sinews and muscles resembles that of the leaden figure from Kampos.[1]

Behind this is a second male figure, who appears to be kneeling on one knee, and holding his right arm forwards, with his fingers and thumb together, as if in the act of sprinkling grain. Immediately behind him is a square block of isodomic masonry, with coping at top, which, from the two-horned object above it, is evidently an altar. It will be shown in the course of this study that this horned adjunct is a usual article of Mycenaean altar furniture.[2]

The altar, with its regular isodomic structure, recalls the limestone walls of some of the better constructed parts of the Palace at Knossos. It probably reproduces the original form of the rectangular altars in its Courts already referred to, of which only the bases now remain.

In striking contrast to the isodomic construction of the altar are the two low walls of the enclosure represented above. Here we see a series of irregular, mostly more or less diamond-shaped, blocks, which may be taken to represent the earlier roughly polygonal style of wall building. It is not possible, however, to be sure whether we have here a rustic survival of the older style, or whether the irregular character of the masonry is intended to indicate that it is of more ancient date than the altar outside. If, as I venture to believe, we have here to deal with the temenos of a sacred grove, the latter hypothesis may appear the more probable.

The tree within is certainly a fig-tree, the characteristic outline of the leaves being clearly defined. On a signet-ring, to be described below,[3] also found on the site of Knossos, a group of sacred trees is seen within the temenos wall of a sanctuary which, from the trifid character of their foliage,

---

[1] Tsuntas, Μυκῆναι, Pl. XI.   [2] See below, p. 37 *seqq.*   [3] See p. 72.

FIG. 2.—FRAGMENT OF STEATITE PYXIS—KNOSSOS.

may also with some probability be recognised as fig-trees. This analogy, coupled with the walled enclosure and the altar in front of it, leads to the conclusion that here too we see before us one of a grove of sacred trees within its sanctuary wall. It is probable that the gold plates in the shape of fig-leaves found in the Acropolis tomb at Mycenae [1]—the thin foil of which proclaims their connexion with funereal cult—are also connected with the special sanctity of this tree.

The traditional sanctity of the fig-tree is well marked in the later cult of Greece. The Sacred Fig, the gift of Demeter, is well known, which stood on the Eleusinian Way beside the tomb of Phytalos, and gave his spirit an undying habitation.[2] Fig-leaves as religious types appear on the coins of Kameiros in Rhodes and of the Carian Idyma. In Laconia Dionysos was worshipped under the form of a fig-tree.[3] A fig-tree is said to have sprung where Gaia sought to ward off the bolts of Zeus from her son Sykeas, and the prophylactic powers of these trees against lightning were well known.[4] The sanctity of the fig-tree among the primitive elements of the Peloponnese, as well as in Mycenaean Crete, will be shown to have a special value in relation to the Ficus Ruminalis at Rome.[5] Both on the score of fruitfulness, and from the character of the spots where it is found, the fig-tree may well have inspired a special veneration in primitive Aegean cult. In Crete it still grows wild where no other tree can fix its roots, at the mouth of the caves of indigenous divinities and in the rocky mountain clefts beside once sacred springs.

The post-like object to the right of the fig-tree in the steatite relief fragment remains enigmatical. It may well be some kind of sacred post or 'Ashera'—perhaps the sacral object which recurs with religious subjects on several Mycenaean gems [6]—an upright post impaling a triangle. The attitude of the man apparently engaged in sprinkling grain in front of the altar seems capable of a very probable explanation. When we recall the fact that the altar, with the same horn-like appendages, that surmounts the small gold shrines from the shaft-graves at Mycenae, is accompanied on either side by two figures of doves, and that the shrines themselves stand in close relation to small gold images of a naked Goddess with doves perched on her head and shoulders, it becomes highly probable that the kneeling man on the cup is engaged in sprinkling grain for sacred birds of the same kind. That the dove had become domesticated in Crete before the great days of Mycenae appears probable from the discovery which I made in an early house beneath the Palace at Knossos of a painted vase in the form of a dove, belonging to the prae-Mycenaean or Kamares class of pottery.

---

[1] Schliemann, *Mycenae*, pp. 191, 192, Figs. 290, 291. These form part of a cruciform ornament. Schliemann did not notice that they were fig-leaves, but their outline is quite naturalistically drawn.

[2] Paus. i. 37.

[3] *Athenaeus*, iii. 14: Διόνυσος Συκίτης. Cf. Bötticher, *Baumkultus*, p. 437.

[4] See Bötticher, *op. cit.* p. 440.

[5] See below, p. 30 *seqq.*

[6] See below, p. 56, Fig. 31.

§ 3.—*The Dove Cult of Primitive Greece.*

It must not be forgotten that birds of various kinds play an important part in this early cult of sacred trees and pillars. Among primitive races at the present day the spiritual being constantly descends on the tree or stone in the form of a bird, or passes from either of them to the votary himself in the same bird form, as the agent of his inspiration.

It is certain that much misconception as to the part played by sacred birds in ancient religion has been produced by the thoroughly unscientific habit of looking for the origin of the associated phenomena through the vista of later highly specialised cults, instead of from the standpoint of primitive ideas. Especially has this been the case with the sacred doves of Greece. Even the dove cult associated with Semiramis was, as has been well pointed out by M. Salomon Reinach,[1] in its origin un-Semitic. Nor in its early stage was there any special connexion with Aphrodîté. In the Odyssey the dove bears nectar to Zeus.[2] His soothsaying wild doves at Dodona go back to the beginnings of Hellenic religion. The dove is equally connected with Dionê, who represented the consort of the 'Pelasgian' Zeus long before she was assimilated with Aphrodîté. It may be noted that where the sacred doves appear in their simplest European form they are generally associated with a sepulchral cult. It is in fact a favourite shape, in which the spirit of the departed haunts his last resting-place, and in accordance with this idea we see the heathen Lombards ornamenting their grave-posts with the effigy of a dove.[3] Nor was it otherwise in prehistoric Cyprus. The figures of doves that adorn the rims of certain vases from the early Copper Age tombs of the island,[4] accompanied with cone-like figures and small libation vases, are most probably connected with a sepulchral cult.

§ 4.—*The Association of Sacred Tree and Pillar.*

In succeeding sections attention will be called to a whole series of Mycenaean cult scenes in which the sacred tree is associated with the sacred pillar. This dual cult is indeed so widespread that it may be said to mark a definite early stage of religious evolution. In treating here of this primitive religious type the cult of trees and pillars, or rude stones, has been regarded as an identical form of worship.[5] The group

---

[1] *Anthropologie*, vi. pp. 562, 563.

[2] *Od.* xii. 62, 63.

[3] Paul Diac. *De Gestis Langobardorum*, v. 34.

[4] Ohnefalsch-Richter, *Kypros, die Bibel und Homer*, p. 283, Figs. 181, 182, 186. Tombs of the early class in which these vases occur go back, if we may judge from the discovery in one of them of a cylinder of Sargon (3800 B.C.), as early as the fourth millennium before our era.

[5] For the ideas underlying this widespread primitive cult I need only refer to Tylor, *Primitive Culture*, ii. p. 160 *seqq.* and p. 215 *seqq.* The spirit is generally forced to enter the stone or pillar by charms and incantations, and sometimes also passes into the body of the priest or worshipper. The 'possession' itself of the material object is only in its nature temporary. 'When the spirit departs the "idol" remains only a sacred object. When a deity is thus brought down into a tree it blends with the tree life.'

is indeed inseparable, and a special feature of the Mycenaean cult scenes with which we have to deal is the constant combination of the sacred tree with pillar or dolmen. The same religious idea—the possession of the material object by the *numen* of the divinity—is common to both. The two forms, moreover shade off into one another; the living tree, as will be seen, can be converted into a column or a tree-pillar, retaining the sanctity of the original. No doubt, as compared with the pillar-form, the living tree was in some way a more realistic impersonation of the godhead, as a depositary of the divine life manifested by its fruits and foliage. In the whispering of its leaves and the melancholy soughing of the breeze was heard, as at Dodona, the actual voice of the divinity. The spiritual possession of the stone or pillar was more temporary in its nature, and the result of a special act of ritual invocation. But the presence of the tree or bush which afforded a more permanent manifestation of divine life may have been thought to facilitate the simultaneous presence of the divinity in the stock or stone, just as both of them co-operate towards the 'possession' of the votary himself.

In India, where worship of this primitive character is perhaps best illustrated at the present day, the collocation of tree and stone is equally frequent. The rough pyramidal pillars of the Bhuta Spirit, the dolmen shrines with their sacred stones, and many other rude "baetyls" of the same kind, such as those of the Horse God and the Village God among the Khonds, are commonly set up beneath holy trees. In the Druidical worship of the West, the tree divinity and the Menhir or stone pillar are associated in a very similar manner, and lingering traditions of their relationship are still traceable in modern folklore. To illustrate indeed this sympathetic conjunction of tree and pillar we have to go no further afield than the borders of Oxfordshire and Warwickshire. Beside the pre-historic stone fence of Rollright the elder tree still stands hard by the King Stone, about which it is told that when the flowery branch was cut on Midsummer Eve, the tree bled, the stone 'moved its head.' [1]

§ 5.—*The 'Labyrinth' and the Pillar Shrines of the God of the Double Axe.*

It will be shown in the course of this study that the cult objects of Mycenaean times almost exclusively consisted of sacred stones, pillars, and trees. It appears, however, that certain symbolic objects, like the double axe, also at times stood as the visible impersonation of the divinity. A valuable illustration of this aspect of primitive cult, which has hitherto escaped attention, is supplied by the subject of a painted Mycenaean vase (Fig. 3), now in the British Museum, found during the recent excavations at Old Salamis in Cyprus.[2] We see here the repeated delineation of a double axe

---

[1] See my paper on 'The Rollright Stones and their Folklore,' p. 20, *Folklore Journal,* 1895.

[2] It is worth noting in this connexion the appearance of a Zeus Labranios in Cyprus. I. H. Hall, *Journ. American Oriental Soc.* 1883. Cited by O. Richter, *Kypros,* &c. p. 21.

apparently set in the ground between pairs of bulls, which also have double axes between their horns. But this representation contains a still more interesting feature. At the foot of the handle of axe, namely, appears in each case that distinctive piece of Mycenaean ritual furniture elsewhere described as 'the horns of consecration.' It occupies the same position in relation to the double axe as in other cases it does to the pillar or tree forms of the divinity. We have here therefore an indication that the double axe itself was an object of worship, and represented the material form or indwelling-place of the divinity, in the same way as his aniconic image of stone or wood. It is a form of worship very similar to that described by Ammianus as still existing in his days among the Alans of the East Pontic coastlands, who simply fixed a naked sword into the ground with barbaric ritual, and worshipped it as the God of War.[1] A curious parallel to this is to be found in a Hittite relief at Pterium,[2] which represents a great sword with the blade stuck in the ground. The handle here has come to life, and portrays the divinity himself and his lion supporters.

FIG. 3.—DOUBLE AXE WITH 'HORNS OF CONSECRATION' BETWEEN BULLS' HEADS WITH SIMILAR AXES, MYCENAEAN VASE, OLD SALAMIS.

The idea of the double axe as the actual material shape of the divinity, the object into which his spiritual essence might enter as it did into his sacred pillar or tree, throws a new light on the scene represented on the large gold signet from the Akropolis treasure at Mycenae (Fig. 4). Here, above the group of the Goddess and her handmaidens, and beneath the conjoined figures of the sun and moon, is seen a double axe, which is surely

---

[1] Amm. Marc. xxxi. 2, 21. 'Nec templum apud eos visitur aut delubrum. . . . sed gladius barbarico ritu humi figitur nudus eumque ut Martem regionum quas circumcircant praesulem verecundius colunt.' Prof. Ernest Gardner also calls my attention to a passage of the Schol. A on Iliad A 264; (Καινεὺς) πήξας ἀκόντιον ἐν τῷ μεσαιτάτῳ τῆς ἀγορᾶς θεὸν τοῦτο προσέταξεν ἀριθμεῖν.

[2] Perrot et Chipiez, L'Art dans l'Antiquité, t. iv. p. 642 and p. 647, Fig. 320.

something more than a mere symbol. It stands in a natural relation to the small figure of the warrior God to the left, and probably represents one of the cult forms under which he was worshipped. The small, apparently descending, image of the God himself may be compared with a similar armed figure on a ring from Knossos, to be described below, in which the cult form of the divinity is seen in the shape of an obelisk. The tree behind the Goddess on the signet-ring, the small stone cairn on which one of the attendants stands and the double axe probably reproduce for us the external aspect of the scene of worship, into which religious fancy has, here, also pictorially introduced the divine actors. The curious reduplication of the axe blades suggests indeed that it stands as an image of the conjunction of the divine pair—a solar and a lunar divinity. This primitive aspect of the cult, in which the double axe was actually regarded as a pair

Fig. 4.—Gold Signet from Akropolis Treasure, Mycenae (¾).

of divinities, receives in fact a curious illustration from the human imagery of later Greek cult. On the reverse of the coins of Tenedos, as on so many Carian types, the old double axe form of the divinity is still preserved, while on the obverse side appears its anthropomorphic equivalent in the shape of a janiform head, which has been identified with Dionysos and Ariadnê.[1] It may be noted that in Tenedos Dionysos is the solar Sabazios of the Thraco-Phrygian cult.

With the evidence of this primitive cult of the weapon itself before our eyes it seems natural to interpret names of Carian sanctuaries like Labranda in the most literal sense as the place of the sacred *labrys*, which was the

[1] Head, *Historia Numorum*, pp. 476, 477.

Lydian (or Carian) name for the Greek πέλεκυς, or double-edged axe.[1] On Carian coins indeed of quite late date the *labrys*, set up on its long pillar-like handle, with two dependent fillets, has much the appearance of a cult image.[2] The name itself reappears in variant forms, and notably connects itself with Labranda near Mylasa, which was a principal scene of the worship of the Carian Zeus. A traditional connexion between the Carian and old Cretan worship is found in the name Labrandos applied to one of the Curetes who was said to have migrated to the neighbourhood of Tralles,[3] and whose associate, moreover, Panamôros preserves another form of the name of the Carian divinity.[4]

The appearance of the divine double axe on the vase between the two bulls finds a close parallel in the Mycenaean lentoid gem from the Heraeum,[5] on which a double axe is seen immediately above a bull's head. The connexion of the God of the Double Axe with the animal is well brought out on the Anatolian side by the figure of Jupiter Dolichenus, a Commagenian variant of the Carian god, who stands, after the old Hittite manner, on the back of the bull. Once more we are taken back to Crete, and to the parallel associations of Zeus-Minos and the Minotaur. These comparisons, moreover, give an extraordinary interest to an identification already arrived at on philological grounds. It was first pointed out by Max Mayer[6] that the Carian Labrandos or Labraundos in its variant forms is in fact the equivalent of the Cretan Labyrinthos. The Cretan Labyrinth is essentially 'the House of the Double Axe.'[7]

---

[1] Plutarch, *Quaest. Graec.* 45.

[2] See especially the reverse of a coin of Aphrodisias, struck under Augustus, *B. M. Cat. Caria,* &c., Pl. VII. 2. Zeus Labraundos is often represented in only partially anthropomorphised form.

[3] *Et. Magn. s.v.* Εὔδωνος. Cf. Roscher's *Lexikon,* Art. 'Kureten,' p. 1599.

[4] Πανάμαρος is the more usual form. See Kretschmer, *Einleitung in d. Gesch. d. griech. Sprache,* p. 303, n. 2.

[5] Schliemann, *Mycenae,* p. 362, Fig. 541; Furtwängler, *Antike Gemmen,* Pl. II. 42.

[6] *Jahrbuch d. K. D. Inst.* vii. (1892), p. 191. He derives Λαβύρινθος from Λαβρύνθιος (Ζεύς), a possible adjectival form of Λάβρυς. A similar but somewhat variant view · is put forth by Kretschmer (*Einleitung,* p. 404), to whom it had occurred independently. He makes Λαβύρινθος a Cretan corruption of the Carian Λαβραυνδος, or its alternative form Λαβραυυνδος. Dr. W. Spiegelberg, indeed, has lately (*Orientalistische Litteratur-Zeitung,* Dec. 1900, pp. 447—449), revived the view, suggested by Jablonsky, that the name Λαβύρινθος took its origin from the Egyptian building known to the Greeks by that name, the Mortuary Temple, namely of Amenemhat III, whose more lasting monu-

ment is the Fayum Province. The official form of Amenemhat's name $N - m;{}^{\prime}t - Re^{\prime}$ was Grecised into Λαβαρίς and Spiegelberg would derive Λαβύρινθος from this + the -ινθος ending of place-names, as Κόρ-ινθος. But the obvious objection to this is that this termination, which in related forms can be traced through a large Anatolian region as well as Greece, belongs to the præ-Hellenic element of the Aegean world, to the same element, in fact, to which *labrys* itself belongs. On the other hand it is quite natural to suppose that the Greeks having taken over the word Λαβύρινθος applied by the earlier race to the Cretan building, should by a kind of *Volksetymologie* transfer the term to the Temple of 'Labaris.'

[7] Max Mayer and Kretschmer (*locc. citt.*) derive the names of the places Λάβρανδα and Λαβύρινθος from the names of the God, and thus *indirectly* from the λάβρυς. But the numerous terminations of local Carian names in -nda -ndos, on the one side, and of præ-Hellenic sites in Greece in -inthos or -yn(th)s, make it probable that both the Labyrinth and Labranda may have taken their name *directly* from the sacred axe, meaning simply "the place of the *labrys*."

In the great prehistoric Palace at present partially excavated by me at Knossos I have ventured on many grounds to recognise the true original of the traditional Labyrinth. It is needless here to speak of its long corridors and succession of magazines with their blind endings, its tortuous passages, and maze of lesser chambers, of the harem scenes painted on its walls, and its huge fresco-paintings and reliefs of bulls, grappled perhaps by men, as on a gem impression from the same site, the Mycenaean prototype of Theseus and the

FIG. 5.—PILLAR OF THE DOUBLE AXES IN PALACE, KNOSSOS.

Minotaur. All this might give a local colour to the mythical scenes with which the building became associated. But there is direct evidence of even a more cogent nature. It was itself the 'House of the Double Axe,' and the Palace was at the same time a sanctuary. The chief corner stones and door-jambs, made of huge gypsum blocks, are incised with the double axe sign, implying consecration to the Cretan Zeus. More than this, in the centre of the building are two small contiguous chambers, in the middle of each of which rises a square column, formed of a series of blocks, on every side of each of which in one case and on three sides of the other is engraved a double axe (Fig. 5). There can, I venture to think, be little doubt that these chambers are shrines, probably belonging to the oldest part of the building, and the pillars thus marked with the sign of the God are in fact his aniconic images. The double axe is thus combined with the sacred pillar.

This view is corroborated by the occurrence in a Mycenaean building excavated by Mr. Hogarth on the opposite hill of Gypsades[1] of a small room with a pillar of the same construction, on either side of which were more or less symmetrically arranged rows of clay cups turned upside down, such as are otherwise so abundantly associated with the votive deposits of the Cretan Cave sanctuaries. In this case the blocks forming the central pillar are not incised with the double axe symbol; but if the addition of any special religious attribute is now wanting, it may originally have been supplied by means of the painted coating of plaster so generally employed in Mycenaean Knossos.

These Cretan pillar shrines find an interesting parallel in two contiguous chambers excavated by the British School at Phylakopi,[2] which were also exceptionally provided with free-standing square pillars. The presence of a curious type of painted vessel of the earlier Aegean class, apparently used for the reception of libations, had already made it probable to the excavators that these columnar chambers should be regarded as shrines. In this case, as probably in the Palace at Knossos, this pillar shrine in its original form goes back to the pre-Mycenaean period. In the presence of the Cretan parallels the full value of the free-standing pillar here as a vehicle of divine presence must now be recognised. It will be shown from a variety of evidence that the most typical form of the Mycenaean sacred pillar is represented as actually performing a structural function, and is in fact a 'Pillar of the House.'

A useful commentary on these more or less domestic pillar shrines of the Mycenaeans is supplied by a vase fragment from a tomb at Enkomi (Old Salamis)[3] in which female votaries are seen within a two-storeyed building, their hands raised in the act of adoration on either side of what appear to be square columns like those in the Knossian chambers (Fig. 6).

The recent exploration of the inner sanctuary of the Diktaean Cave has produced an interesting discovery which may be taken to illustrate the Mycenaean pillar worship in its most primitive and naturalistic form. In the lower vault of the Cave, and partly out of the waters of its subterranean pool, rises a forest of stalactite columns, stuck into the crevices of which Mr. Hogarth found hundreds of votive bronzes, and among them a quantity of double axes declaring the special dedication to the Cretan Zeus. In these votive objects, thrust into the crevices of the stalactite, we may, I venture to think, see something more than a convenient way of disposing of offerings. They clearly indicate

---

[1] See *Annual of the British School at Athens*, 1900.

[2] *Annual of the British School at Athens*,

1897–8, p. 15.

[3] A. S. Murray, etc. *Excavations in Cyprus*, p. 73, Fig. 127.

that in this case the natural columns of this Cavern shrine were regarded as the baetylic forms of the divinity, just as the Cave itself is here his temple. It may be observed, moreover, in this connexion that some of the shorter stalagmitic formations of this 'Holy of Holies' are perfect representations of the omphalos type, and perhaps supply the true explanation of the origin of this form of sacred stone.

It will be shown in the succeeding section that the inscribed libation table found in the upper sanctuary of the same Cave is in a similar way associated with a baetylic form of the God as an artificial column or cone.

§ 6.—*The βαίτυλος and Baetylic Tables of Offering.*

There will be repeated occasion for observing the close correspondence of the Mycenaean and Semitic cult of sacred pillars.   The best known

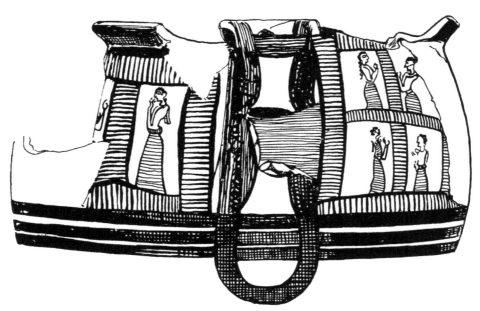

Fig. 6.—Pillar Shrines and Votaries on Vase Fragment from Old Salamis, Cyprus.

instance of the kind is the pillar set up by Jacob, which was literally Bethel, the House of God.   It has been suggested that these Semitic words, or some parallel form of the same—indicating the stone as the temporary place of indwelling for a divinity—supplied the Greeks with the term βαίτυλος or βαιτύλιον,[1] and applied in a special way to the stone which, according to the

---

[1] Lenormant, Art. 'Baetylia' in Daremberg and Saglio, *Dict. des Antiquités*, i. 642 *seqq.*; Baudissin, *Studien zur Semitischen Religion*, ii. 232 *seqq.*; Dr. H. Lewy, *Die Semitischen Fremdwörter im Griechischen*, pp. 255, 256, who prefers the derivation '*bet 'eloah*.' The word was derived by the ancient grammarians from the Cretan βαίτη = goat or goat-skin, in

Cretan legend, was swallowed by Kronos under the belief that it was his son. But this stone, as Lenormant has well pointed out, is in fact nothing else than the material form of the Cretan Zeus himself.   The name was equally applied to the black cone representing the Sun God at Baalbec.[1]

In the stalactite pillars of the inner sanctuary of the great Diktaean Cave with their votive double axes, the emblems of the Cretan Zeus, we have already ventured to recognise baetylic shapes of the God in a purely natural form. But, over and above this, there remains a remarkable piece of evidence which assuredly implies the existence of an artificial pillar image of the divinity, it may be even the actual 'baetylos' of remote tradition.

In the great upper hall of the Cave, near the small temenos more recently explored by the late Director of the British School, was found the fragment of a steatite table with cup-like receptacles for libations, and bearing upon it part of a prehistoric inscription, described by me in a previous publication.[2]   The evidence of a triple libation was there compared with the old Arcadian rite, the offering to the Dead before the falls of Styx.[3]

$$\Pi \rho \hat{\omega} \tau \alpha \ \mu \epsilon \lambda \iota \kappa \rho \acute{\eta} \tau \omega, \ \mu \epsilon \tau \acute{\epsilon} \pi \epsilon \iota \tau \alpha \ \delta \grave{\epsilon} \ \acute{\eta} \delta \acute{\epsilon} \ddot{\iota} \ o \emph{\i} \nu \omega,$$
$$T \grave{o} \ \tau \rho \acute{\iota} \tau o \nu \ \alpha \hat{\upsilon} \theta' \ \emph{\"u} \delta \alpha \tau \iota.$$

The special appropriateness was pointed out of such a rite in the case of the Cave shrine of the infant Zeus, where, according to the legend, he had been fed by the Nymphs with mingled milk and honey.[4]   But there remains another feature of the Libation Table which brings it into still closer relation with the primitive baetylic image of the God.

The slab of offering, in this case, with its triple receptacle, is in fact a part of a table.   Its angles on the under side show projections which fitted on to four legs.   But over and above these corner supports, which for a table of such dimensions would have been amply sufficient, the under surface of the offertory slab also displays a larger circular prominence, which shows that it was set over a small central column.   The analysis of the original cult object now becomes clear.   The Table of Offerings itself is only a secondary feature.   The slab with the cups for libation was simply placed over the pillar,—here, perhaps, as shown in the reconstruction of the whole in Fig. 7, of slightly conical outline,—which in fact represents the aniconic image of the divinity, the actual *baetylos* of Zeus.

The corner posts of the libation table were only added to afford additional security ; they give to the whole the appearance of a small shrine resembling the Mycenaean pillar shrines to be described in succeeding

---

special allusion to the stone substitute of Zeus swallowed by Kronos. This view has been revived by Svoronos, *Zeitschrift für Numismatik*, 1888, p. 222, and is preferred by Maximilian Mayer, Art. 'Kronos,' in Roscher's *Lexikon*, ii. p. 1,524. But it is not explained how the word came to be applied (according to the *Etymol. M.*) to the stone of

Heliopolis.

[1] *Etymol. Mag.* s. v.

[2] 'Further Discoveries of Cretan and Aegean Script,' *J.H.S.* xvii. (1897) p. 350 *seqq.*

[3] *Od.* x. 519, 520.

[4] Cf. Diod. v. 20.

sections.[1] In a sense, too, the table here has a real analogy with these, the top slab of such baetylic shrines being used either as a resting place for votive objects or as the support of a Mycenaean altar. It is to be noted, however, that in both cases the centre of the whole religious construction is the aniconic image within. The term 'altar,' which has been so usually applied to these Mycenaean structures, is quite inadequate, though, as we shall see, these baetylic tables gave rise in later days, when the aniconic image itself had been superseded, to a Cretan form of altar, and to certain types of tripod.

In the most primitive form of this pillar cult the offerings are simply

FIG. 7.—BAETYLIC TABLE OF OFFERING FROM THE DIKTAEAN CAVE, RESTORED.

placed on the holy stone.[2] In other cases a basket or some temporary receptacle is laid on top of it, containing the offering. Thus, for example, in a Greco-Roman relief,[3] the shovel-shaped basket of Bacchus—the Liknos or

---

[1] The analogy between these and the Diktaean Libation Table as reconstructed has been noted by Dr. P. Wolters (*Jahrbuch d. k. d. Inst.* 1900, pp. 147, 148); but the explanation given by him, that both the Diktaean structure and those represented on the signets are 'altars,' falls, as I venture to believe, short of the truth. The view again and again put forward in the course of the present study, is that they are in reality small shrines, the central columnar support of which

is the aniconic image of the divinity. They are only 'altars' in a secondary sense.

[2] I have actually seen egg offerings thus placed on the top of a sacred stone in Finnish Lapland. The stone itself was so high that for the convenience of the votaries a primitive form of ladder in the shape of a notched pine trunk was laid against it.

[3] *Mon. Inediti*, ii. Pl. 37; Bötticher, *Baum-kultus*, Pl. 56.

Vannus—laden with grapes and other fruit, is placed on the coniform summit of a divine pillar, which, as is so often the case, is associated with a holy tree and sacral arch. It is interesting to note that the most typical form of the Hittite altars represents the superposition of a receptacle of the same shape as this offertory-basket on what must certainly be recognised as a baetylic cone (Fig. 8 a). In other cases the same conical base supports a small flat slab with offerings upon it (Fig. 8 b),

FIG. 8.—BAETYLIC CONES AND OFFERING SLABS ON HITTITE SEALS.

and at times again it is simply surmounted by a rayed disk indicative of the divinity of the stone (Fig. 8 c).[1] The cup-shaped receptacles of the Diktaean slab represent, in a more developed form, the cup-like hollows worked for the reception of offerings in the capstones of some of our Dolmens, which themselves served as the shrines of departed human spirits.

FIG. 9.—SMALL BAETYLIC ALTAR FROM CYRENAICA.

A very interesting parallel to the baetylic libation table of the Diktaean Cave is supplied from a quarter which has perhaps a special significance in connexion with the primitive monuments of Cretan religion. The Libyan God Zeus Ammon was represented in his oracular shrine of the Oasis as a kind of cone or omphalos, a survival of aniconic worship which recalls the obelisk of his Egyptian impersonation, Amen-Ra. But a limestone object (Fig. 9) obtained by Dr. Dennis in the Cyrenaica [2] reproduces the essential features of the pillar table of the Diktaean Cave. The central column is here of conical form, which on Libyan soil we should naturally connect with the native Zeus. The table above has the four subsidiary legs of the Cretan type, while its upper surface is surmounted by a kind of receptacle open

---

[1] Figs. 8 a, and 8 b, Tarsus seal, haematite, *Arch. Inst. Journ.* 1887, p. 348 (Ashmolean Museum); cf. cylindrical seal from Cæsarea in Cappadocia, Dresden Museum (L. Messerschmidt, *Orientalistische Litteratur-Zeitung,* 1900, p. 442, Fig. 1). Fig. 8, c, seal from Yüzgat, S.E. of Boghaz Kiöi, Budge, *Proc. Soc, Bibl. Arch.* ix. Nov. 1886,

(in the British Museum). Cf. another seal from Yüzgat (T. Tyler, *Internat. Congr. of Orientalists,* 1892, p. 267, Fig. 13), where the winged disk surmounts a somewhat more primitive cone. On several examples the God himself is seen in anthropomorphic form before his baetylic cone and altar slab.

[2] Now in the British Museum. Mr. Dennis

on one side, and in this respect resembling the basket or Vannus placed on the sacred pillar already described.

It is possible that the cult object from the Cyrenaica is of considerably later date than that from the Diktaean Cave, but there can be no doubt as to the parallelism presented by its constituent parts. Here, too, we have, —moulded, it is true, into a single piece,—the central object of worship, in this case a sacred cone, with the table placed above it and the receptacle for offerings on the upper surface.

Two interesting pieces of evidence seem to show that this baetylic table formed a special feature in the indigenous Cretan cult, and even survived to Roman times. On a Mycenaean lentoid gem found in Crete, and presenting in a variant form the Lions' Gate type,[1] the sacred object on which the forefeet of the animals rest is neither the columnar image nor the usual Mycenaean altar with incurving sides, but an object consisting of a short central column, with a slab above it, further supported by side legs (Fig. 10). Here once more we recognise the essential features of the offertory table placed above the sacred pillar.

FIG. 10.—BAETYLIC TABLE USED AS A BASE FOR SACRAL LIONS ON CRETAN GEM.

FIG. 11.—BAETYLIC ALTAR ON COIN OF CRETAN COMMUNITY.

In a much later shape, and with the original idea of the pillar idol merged in the sanctity of the whole block as a vehicle of offering, we find the same religious element surviving in a form of altar which occurs on certain coins of the Cretan community[2] as a badge of their common worship. On these coins (Fig. 11), struck under the Roman dominion, and bearing in an abbreviated form the legend ΚΟΙΝΟΝ ΚΡΗΤΩΝ, we still clearly distinguish the central baetylic column and the offertory slab above, with the legs at its angles. The table itself is here surmounted by a central akroterion, and lateral excrescences which represent here, as elsewhere, the tradition of the typical cult object of Mycenaean times, 'the horns of consecration.'

---

obtained it when Consul at Bengazi, but no account exists of the exact place or circumstances of its discovery.

[1] More fully described below. See p. 63.
[2] Svoronos, *Numismatique de la Crète ancienne*, Pl. XXXV. 36.

Some impressed glass plaques recently found by Dr. Tsuntas in tombs of the Lower Town at Mycenae[1] supply three different examples of the ancient pillar cult in association with the strange lion-headed daemons of Mycenaean religion.[2] Elsewhere[3] we have seen the same monsters in the ritual act of watering the nurseling palms. In the present case they are engaged in pouring libations over sacred stones and pillars. In Fig. 12,[4] we see them holding the usual prochous vases, or beaked ewers, over what appears to be a cairn formed of natural stones, with a larger block on the top. This primitive form of stone worship recalls the setting up of stones from the bed of the Jordan by Jacob at Gilgal. It also receives a possible illustration in the stone heap on which a small figure stands in the scene presented by the great signet from Mycenae. In Fig. 13[5] the same daemons are similarly engaged on either side of square pillars, which in form recall those with the incised double axes

FIG. 12.—IMPRESSED GLASS PLAQUE FROM MYCENAE: DAEMONS POURING LIBATIONS ON SACRED CAIRN.

in the Palace of Knossos. The third example (Fig. 14)[6] is of a somewhat different kind, and supplies a most interesting analogy to the 'baetylic table' described above.

Here the ritual libation is poured into what appears to be a kind of bowl,[7] resting on a column of the Mycenaean architectural type, decreasing in

FIG. 13.—IMPRESSED GLASS PLAQUE FROM MYCENAE: DAEMONS POURING LIBATIONS ON SACRED PILLAR.

FIG. 14.—IMPRESSED GLASS PLAQUE FROM MYCENAE: DAEMONS POURING LIBATIONS ON A BAETYLIC TRIPOD-LEBÊS.

diameter towards its base. The bowl has two further supports on either side, answering to the legs of the offertory slab in the types above described. It

---

[1] Thanks to the kindness of Dr. Tsuntas I am able to reproduce these objects from drawings made by M. Gilliéron.

[2] See below, p. 70 *seqq.*

[3] See Fig. 1, p. 3.

[4] From a dromos tomb, with rock-cut square chamber, some distance north of the Acropolis.

[5] Found in a plundered tholos tomb west of

the ridge leading from the Acropolis to Charvati.

[6] Found in the same tomb as the preceding.

[7] Dr. Tsuntas interprets this feature in the same manner. It might be also regarded as a capital of the column, but this would not explain the side supports. It is obviously a receptacle

is possible that in this case there were only three legs, and that what we see
before us is in fact a tripod with a central stem. This religious type again
supplies the prototype of a class of tripods that survived to later times, where it
also assumes an anthropomorphic form. The interior baetylic pillar indeed
could hardly be thus treated, and the anthropomorphic element was transferred to the outer supports. A well known example of this kind is supplied
by the Oxford tripod,[1] in which the basin, in addition to its central stem, is
supported by three figures of Goddesses standing on the backs of lions. In a
zoomorphic form the same underlying idea is illustrated by the three serpents
of bronze, which formed the central prop of the golden tripod dedicated to
the Delphian God out of the spoils of the battle of Plataea.[2]

§ 7.—*Zeus Kappôtas and the Meteoric Element in Baetylic Stones.*

The sanctity of baetylic stones and pillars is due to a variety of causes.
It may be connected with some particular manifestation supposed to be of a
spiritual nature—to the interpretation of a sign, or of a dream, as in the case of
Jacob's pillar. Artificial pillars may owe their indwelling spiritual being to
the holiness of the spot where they are set up, to religious symbols like the
double axe carved on their surface, or to some special rite of consecration, of
which, in Mycenaean religion, the two-horned cult object set before them is
often the external symbol. Wooden columns, as we shall see, often take over
their sanctity from the sacred tree out of which they are hewn.

There is also a good deal of evidence to show that certain natural blocks
derived their baetylic qualities from the fact that they were of meteoric origin.
According to Sanchoniathon[3] 'Baetylos' is 'the son of Ouranos,' in other words
sky-fallen. The phenomena associated with aerolites seem indeed to a certain
extent to have attached themselves to the whole class of sacred stones. The
early cults of the Greek world supply a good illustration of this class of ideas in
the 'rude stone,' or ἀργὸς λίθος, that stood near Gythion in Laconia, and was
known as Zeus Kappôtas—in other words the Zeus 'fallen down' from heaven.[4]
Allied to this are the *keraunia* or thunderstones, which, as the 'bolts of
heaven,' were naturally recognised in the stone axes of an earlier age.[5] A
stone found near Mantineia bears an archaic inscription,[6] which shows that

---

[1] See Prof. P. Gardner, *J.H.S.* xvi. (1896)
Pl. XII. and p. 275 *seqq.*, where various
classical parallels to this type of tripod are
given.

[2] Herodotus (ix. 81) speaks of the tripod as
standing over the three-headed serpent.

[3] P. 30, Ed. Orelli.

[4] See Sam Wide, *Lakonische Culte*, p. 21.
'Zeus Kappotas is der vom Himmel gefallene
ἀργὸς λίθος καππώτας = κατα-πώτ-ας aus der
Wurzel πετ-, πώτ-, vgl. πώτ-ά-ομαί.' Sam
Wide saw in it rather a 'thunder-stone' than
meteorite. But the two ideas can hardly

be kept distinct.

[5] Pliny, *H. N.* xxxvii. 9. Sotacus et alia
duo genera fecit cerauniae, nigrae rubentisque,
ac similes eas esse securibus; iis quae nigrae
sunt et rotundae urbes expugnari et classes
easque betulos vocari: quae vero longae sunt
ceraunias.' *Betuli* are βαίτυλοι. On stone
axes or celts regarded as thunderbolts, cf.
J. Evans, *Ancient Stone Implements* (2nd ed.),
p. 62 *seqq.*

[6] Διὸς κεραυνō, Cauer, *Del.* (2nd Ed.) 447,
(*I. G. A.* 101) S. Wide, *loc. cit.*, refers to this.

Zeus himself could be personified as such a stone. The rude stone images of the Charites at Orchomenos were sky-fallen; and a kindred form of the belief is found in the case of the still half aniconic image of ‘the Diana of the Ephesians,’ ‘that fell down from Jupiter.’ It is certain that the religious effect of the descent of a meteorite must have been very great in primitive societies,[1] and may indeed be regarded as the actual origin of certain local cults. But the idea of rude stones as the indwelling place of divinities or spirits was far too universal to be traced to this single source. The meteoric element must rather be regarded as a contributory influence, whence certain features in the beliefs regarding baetylic stones were derived. The idea of their flying through the air or falling from heaven, and their supposed power of burning with inner fire and shining in the night-time, were probably suggested by the phenomena associated with meteoric stones.

§ 8.—*Sepulchral Stelae as Baetylic Habitations of Departed Spirits.*

The stage in aniconic worship in which the pillar is of a purely artificial kind and the stone is, as it were, offered to a spiritual being as a place of habitation, marks an advance on the more primitive idea of a holy stone as one that has in some way manifested itself as being in spiritual possession. Yet the rites by which the medicine men of primitive races the world over are able to shut up Gods or Spirits in a material object, show how easily the idea of attracting or compelling such spiritual occupation must have arisen. A proof of this is found in the ideas attaching to the rude stone monuments placed over graves. These have not merely a memorial significance, but are actually a place of indwelling for the ghosts of the occupant of the tomb or his followers and slaves. It is before the dead in his stony form that due offerings of food and drink are placed; and when the monument takes a human shape, such as in a grosser form is assumed by the Kammennaye Babe that rise above the Kurgans of the Russian Steppes, or in a more artistic guise is seen in the funereal reliefs of Sparta, the deceased himself is often represented holding in his hands the cup for libations. The stelae of the graves at Mycenae must themselves be regarded as baetylic forms of the departed spirits of members of the royal house; and in the reliefs upon them exhibiting scenes of war and the chase we may recognise a compromise between the idea of supplying a spirit with an aniconic habitation, and that of pictorially delineating it in human form, of which we shall see numerous illustrations in Mycenaean cult scenes.

§ 9.—*The Tomb of Zeus.*

The two conceptions of the pillar image of divinity and of the tombstone as the dwelling place of a departed spirit meet in the idea of a mortal God.

---

[1] See Prof. H. A. Miers, ‘The Fall of Meteorites in Ancient and Modern Times,’ *Science Progress*, vol. vii. 1898.

In some respects later traditions of this class may be due to the mere attempt to explain the presence of an aniconic image of divinity in days when anthropomorphic forms had triumphed. But the very ancient religious elements with which traditions of this class are often bound up point to a time when the God himself could be regarded as having run an earthly course, and passed like an ordinary mortal through the gates of death.

We are tempted to believe that some of the small cellular shrines, illustrated by the signet rings of the Mycenaeans, were themselves derived from analogous forms of a primitive sepulchral architecture such as we find in the megalithic dolmen chamber of Mycenae itself, and the analogous structure belonging to the prae-Mycenaean or 'Amorgian' period of Aegean culture lately excavated at Chalandrianê in Syra.[1]

The survival of such sepulchral traditions in connexion with divinities is very widespread on Greek, Syrian and Anatolian ground. The tomb of Adonis was placed within the temple-court of Byblos. In that of Paphos the grave of Aphroditê was pointed out as well as her sacred cone,[2] and with it was the burial-place of her chosen priest, the hero Kinyras,[3] a favourite or double of Apollo, otherwise akin to the Cilician Sandon. The omphalos of Apollo at Delphi became known as 'the tomb of Dionysos'[4]—who, under his earlier Thracian form of Sabazios, was himself a Sun-God—and was even said to bear an inscription parodied from that of the Cretan Zeus.[5] At other times it was the Pythôn's tomb.

This solar aspect of Dionysos gives a special value to the fact that at Argos the 'tomb of Ariadnê' was shown in the sanctuary of the Cretan Dionysos.[6] In the sacred grove of Aphroditê Ariadnê at Amathus in Cyprus was also shown her tomb.[7]

At Amyklae, where, as we now know from Tsuntas's excavations, the local cult goes back to Mycenaean antiquity,[8] the colossal image of Apollo, which even in classical times had only partially lost its original aniconic form, stood on its altar seat above the grave of his favourite Hyakinthos. But Hyakinthos himself simply represents the local God of Amyklae in a reduplicated form, and the Laconian colonists, who transferred his tomb and cult to Tarentine soil, regarded Apollo and Hyakinthos as one and the same divinity.[9] In the days when the cult images of the Gods had taken human forms the aniconic idol ceased to be generally intelligible to the worshippers, and its occasional survival side by side with the anthropomorphic impersonation of the divinity led to a revival of the sepulchral tradition in another form. The sacred cone was supposed to mark the burial place of some

---

[1] Tsuntas, 'Εφ. 'Αρχ. 1899, Pl. VII.

[2] Clem. Rom. *Recogn.* 1. 24; Enmann, *Kypros und der Ursprung des Aphroditekultus*, p. 34.

[3] Clem. Alex. *Protr.* p. 40; see Enmann, *op. cit.* p. 33 and p. 27 *seqq.*

[4] Tatian, *adv. Graec.* 8, 25. Ὁ δὲ ὀμφαλὸς τάφος ἐστὶ Διονύσου.

[5] Philoch. fr. 22 in Malala, ἔστιν ἰδεῖν τὴν ταφὴν αὐτοῦ ἐν Δελφοῖς παρὰ τὸν Ἀπόλλωνα 'ὁ

χρυσοῦν. βόθρον δέ τι εἶναι ὑπονοεῖται ἡ σορός, ἐν ᾧ γράφεται· 'Ενθάδε κεῖται θανὼν Διόνυσος ὁ ἐκ Σεμέλης.

[6] Paus. ii. 23, 7.

[7] Plutarch, *Theseus*, 20.

[8] 'Εκ τοῦ 'Αμυκλαίου. ['Εφημ. 'Αρχαιολ. 1892, p. 1 *seqq.*]

[9] Cf. Polybios, 1. viii. c. 30, 2.

associated hero or mythical being, in reality simply representing a dual type of the God himself.

But the conception of the mortal God and the cult of his sepulchral monument is most familiar in the abiding traditions of the Cretan Zeus. The 'tomb of Zeus' was shown in Crete down to at least the fourth century of our era, and it was indeed the preservation of this piece of primitive religion, so foreign to later notions, that gained for the Cretans the distinguishing epithet applied to them by Kallimachos[1] and St. Paul. Possibly more than one locality claimed to possess the sepulchre, as the records preserved of it sometimes seem to couple it with the Cave of Zeus on Mount Ida. sometimes with Knossos. Lactantius places it at Knossos, and adds that it bore the inscription in early Greek characters, Zeus, son of Kronos[2]; but according to one version, which clearly fits on to the prae-Hellenic tradition of the island, the original name on the tomb was that of Minôs.[3] According to one legend Pythagoras was said to have written on the tomb:

$$\text{῝Ωδε θανὼν κεῖται Ζᾶν ὃν Δία κικλήσκουσιν.}^{4}$$

Lucian speaks of a tomb and stele[5] and the continued veneration of the monument is attested by Christian writers down to Julius Firmicus,[6] who wrote in the first half of the fourth century. After this there is a break in the written records till the eleventh century, when Michael Psellos speaks of the legend as still living, and relates that the Cretans show a cairn or heap of stones above the grave of Zeus.[7] This might be taken to show that the older monument was then a heap of ruins. It is certain that later Cretan tradition has persistently connected the tomb of Zeus with Mount Juktas which rises as the most prominent height on the land side above the site of Knossos.[8] Personal experiences obtained during two recent explorations of this peak go far to confirm this tradition. All that is not precipitous of the highest point of the ridge of Juktas is enclosed by a 'Cyclopean' wall of

---

[1] Hymn i. :—
Κρῆτες ἀεὶ ψεῦσται, καὶ γὰρ τάφον, ὦ ἄνα, σεῖο
Κρῆτες ἐπεκτήναντο· σὺ δ' οὐ θάνες, ἐσσὶ γὰρ ἀεί.

[2] De Falsa Religione, lib. i. c. 11. 'Sepulchrum eius (sc. Jovis) est in oppido Gnoso. . . . inque sepulchro inscriptum antiquis literis Graecis ὁ Ζεὺς τοῦ Κρόνου.'

[3] Schol. in Callimachum. Hymn. i. According to this version the original description was Μίνωος τοῦ Διὸς τάφος—then the name of Minôs was omitted. This version may, of course, be set down to Euhemerism, but it seems to record a true religious process by which the cult of Minôs passed into that of Zeus. That this explanation should have obtained currency is another indication that a tomb of Zeus was shown at or near Knossos.

[4] Porphyr. v. Pyth. § 17. Cf. Chrysostom

in Ep. Pauli ad Tit. 3. Hoeck, Creta, iii. p. 36. The passages relating to the tomb of Zeus are collected in Meursius, Creta, p. 80.

[5] Jupit. Tragoed. 45: τάφον τινὰ ἐκεῖθι δείκνυσθαι καὶ στήλην ἐφεστάναι. Cf., too, De Sacrificiis, 13.

[6] De Errore Profanarum Religionum, c. vii. 6, A vanis Cretensibus adhuc mortui Jovis tumulus adoratur.

[7] Ἀναγωγὴ εἰς τὸν Τάνταλον, cited by Meursius, Creta : ἐπὶ τῷ τάφῳ δεικνύουσι κολωνόν. Buondelmonti and other later writers refer to the tomb as above a cavern.

[8] Dr. Joseph Hazzidakis, the President of the Cretan Syllogos at Candia, and now Ephor of Antiquities, informs me that the remains on the top of Mount Juktas are still known to the country people about as Μνῆμα τοῦ Ζιά.

large roughly oblong blocks,[1] and within this enclosure, especially towards the summit, the ground is strewn with pottery dating from Mycenaean to Roman times, and including a large number of small cups of pale clay exactly resembling those which occur in votive deposits of Mycenaean date in the caves of Dikta and of Ida, also intimately connected with the cult of the Cretan Zeus. No remains of buildings are visible in this inner area, which tends to show that the primitive enclosure was the temenos of a sanctuary, rather than a walled city. On the uppermost platform of rock, however, are remains of a building constructed with large mortarless blocks of which the ground-plan of part of two small chambers can be roughly traced. A little further on the ridge is the small church of Aphendi Kristos, or the Lord Christ, a name which in Crete clings in an especial way to the ancient sanctuaries of Zeus [2] and marks here in a conspicuous manner the diverted but abiding sanctity of the spot. Popular tradition, the existing cult, and the archaeological traces point alike to the fact that there was here a 'holy sepulchre' of remote antiquity.

Attention will be called below to the scenes on two of the signet rings from Mycenae which certainly seem to point to a funereal cult of some heroic or divine personage, whose shield in one case is suspended to a shr ne beside his pillar image.[3] It is possible that the Mycenaean shield itself, which so often appears as a symbol in the field of gems and signets, at times represents, like the double axe, the aniconic embodiment of the divinity or departed hero. The shield borne by the warrior God on Mycenaean paintings and engraved rings passes naturally to his orgiastic worshippers, the Curetes or Corybantes of later cult. In the case of their Italian counterparts the Salii—the orgiastic priesthood of ancient Rome— the actual form of the Mycenaean shield is preserved in the Ancilia,[4] which were themselves possessors of divine powers of movement and of warning clangour.[5] The first Ancile was 'sky-fallen' like a baetylic stone.

§ 10.—*Small Dimensions of the Mycenaean Shrines.*

The shrines of such a baetylic form of worship as the Mycenaean are naturally small. In some cases we have seen a mere offertory slab, with its

---

[1] The spot was visited by Pashley (*Travels in Crete*, i. p. 252 *seqq.*) who gives a sketch of a part of the outer temenos wall. He also found the spot locally known as the 'Tomb of Zeus.' The best account of the circuit wall is that given by Dr. Antonio Taramelli, 'Ricerche Archeologiche Cretesi,' p. 70 *seqq.* (*Mon. Ant.* vol. ix. 1899), accompanied by plans and illustrations. I cannot find, however, in either writer any mention of the remains of the small building on the summit.

[2] See *Academy*, June 20, 1896, p. 513. The eastern and western ranges of Dikta, the sites respectively of the Temple and Cave of Zeus, are known as the Aphendi Vouno, from

Αὐθέντης Χριστός, or 'Christ the Lord.' A votive deposit, apparently connected with some Zeus cult, on a peak of Lasethi is also known as Aphendi Christos. It is, perhaps, worth noting in this connexion that at 'Minôan' Gaza Zeus Krêtagenês was known as Marnas, a form of the Syrian word for 'Lord.'

[3] See below, p. 79, 82.

[4] This comparison has been independently made by Mr. Warde Fowler, *The Roman Festivals*, p. 350. A similar shield, as Mr. G. F. Hill points out, is carried by the Juno of Lanuvium on Roman denarii.

[5] Liv. *Epit.* lxviii.

corner props, placed above the stone.   In a succeeding section attention will be called to the sacred pillar placed beneath an arch or doorway or beneath the capstone of a kind of dolmen cell.   To such primitive shrines, based on the megalithic chambers of a sepulchral cult, parallels can be found in various parts of the world.   It will be shown, for instance, in the course of this study that the Indian dolmen cells with the baetylic stones set up within them, and the ancient megalithic shrines, such as those of Hagiar Kim and Giganteja in the Maltese Islands or the Balearic Talyots, present a close analogy to the Mycenaean type in which the pillar itself acts as an additional support to the roof-stones.   Of these baetylic cells the dove-shrines of the Akropolis tomb at Mycenae, with their triple division and summit altars, present a somewhat more complex type.   A still further development of this tripartite shrine is now supplied by a fresco painting from the Palace of Knossos representing a small temple, largely of wood-work construction, in which the columns are clearly indicated as aniconic images by the 'horns of consecration' placed beside them and at their feet.   A detailed description of this Mycenaean temple is reserved for a later section.[1]

But even this, the most elaborate example of a Mycenaean sanctuary, is of small dimensions, as is shown by the human figures beside it and the horns within.   The religious ideas indeed associated with this aniconic cult were far removed from those that produced the spacious temples of later times.   The sepulchral chambers, the abode of departed spirits, supplied a much nearer analogy, and the true germ of their development.   Of anthropomorphic temple images there is as yet no trace, and it was not necessary, as in later times, to accommodate the God with a palatial dwelling, which was in fact the glorified *megaron* of mortal kings.   It is doubtless owing to the small dimensions of the Mycenaean shrines that up to the date of the recent Cretan discoveries so little trace has been found of places of worship among the monumental records of this period.   A sacred tree too, it must be remembered, leaves no mark; its sanctuary is hypaethral, and the surrounding enclosure often of rustic construction.

§ 11.—*Aniconic Cult Images Supplemented by Pictorial Representations of Divinities : Transitions to Anthropomorphism.*

It has been remarked above that there is as yet no indication of temple images in human form.   It is true that a certain number of figures appear on the Mycenaean religious designs, which may with great probability be taken to portray the divine personages themselves, rather than their worshippers.   But it may safely be said that we have here to do with creations of religious fancy, rather than with the actual objects of cult.   The idols remained aniconic, but the Gods themselves were naturally pictured to the mind of their worshippers under a more or less human aspect.   It is probable that if more

---

[1] See p. 94 *seqq.*

of the Mycenaean paintings had been preserved, something like a complete view of this imaginative side of the religion might have been unfolded to us. Apart from the minor relics to which we shall presently turn, the only real indication of a cult scene is supplied by the painting on the stucco tablet found in a private house at Mycenae, in which two female adorants stand facing on either side an altar, by which is the figure of an armed God, protected by a great 8-shaped body-shield.[1] A figure of a God with rayed shoulders, holding a similar body-shield, also occurs on a painted ossuary from Milato, in Crete.[2] So, too, a fragment of a fresco from Mycenae itself also reproduces some of the strange Mycenaean daemons.[3] Considering how very little has reached us of the pictorial art of this period, these surviving illustrations of religious subjects, as seen on these paintings, and still more on the signet rings, may be taken to indicate that in this way the outward forms of the Gods and their surroundings were fixed and familiarised by the Mycenaean artists long before they actually affected the shape of the cult images. Here the Gods or other supernatural beings stood portrayed as they were described in hymns and incantations, haunting their sacred seats, feasting in their celestial groves and gardens, or descending at the prayer of the votaries before their sacred pillars and altar-stones. On the Knossian ring already referred to a remarkable illustration will be found of this dual conception of divinity in its human and its pillar form.[4] There an armed God is seen descending in front of his sacred obelisk, before which the votary stands in the attitude of adoration. It is the artist's attempt to express the spiritual being, duly brought down by ritual incantation, so as temporarily to possess its stony resting-place. Elsewhere we see the figure of a Goddess seated beside or even upon her rustic shrine, or, as in the case of the great signet ring from Mycenae, beneath her sacred tree, and tended by her hand-maidens. In other cases, as in the Lions' Gate scheme, we see the pillar image between its guardian monsters replaced on other parallel types by a male or female divinity.[5]

The coexistence of this more realistic imagery side by side with the material objects of primitive cult certainly betrays elements of transition. We discern already foreshadowings of the time, not far distant, when the mental conception of individual divinities would leave its impress on the rude stock or stone or more artistically shaped pillar which from time to time was supposed to become possessed with its spiritual essence. It is true, as already noticed, that the great mass of the small figurines of bronze and clay found in votive deposits of Mycenaean age must probably be regarded as representing the votary himself or his belongings, who were thus placed in the hands of the divinity. But it is by no means impossible that some exceptions exist to this rule, due perhaps in the first instance to the influence of Egyptian or Oriental practice. There is, for

---

[1] Ἐφημερὶς Ἀρχαιολογική, 1887, Pl. X. 2, and p. 162; Tsuntas and Manatt, *Myc. Age*, Pl. XI., p. 299.

[2] See below, p. 76.

[3] Ἐφημερὶς Ἀρχαιολογική, 1887, Pl. X. 1.

[4] See below, p. 72.

[5] See below, p. 65 *seqq*.

example, a fair presumption in favour of the view that certain specialised figures such as the bronze statuettes from Tiryns and Mycenae published by Schliemann may actually portray divinities and have partaken of the nature of cult images. To these two examples from Greek soil may now be added two more belonging to the same type, one of bronze found in the votive stratum of the Cave of Hermês Kranaios, near Sybrita in Crete (Fig. 15) the other of silver found near Nezero, on the borders of Thessaly and Macedonia [1] (Fig. 16). The statuettes in question unquestionably show a close family likeness to certain North Syrian or ' Hittite' bronzes.[2] They have been supposed to represent imported fabrics from the same Oriental source ; but their style is superior to that of the contemporary Syrian bronzes, and their more naturalistic forms proclaim them to be of true Mycenaean workmanship. Their characteristic attitude, as well as the Egyptianising helmet, brings them in close relation to the figures of Resheph, the Semitic Lightning God, on Egyptian monuments.[3] A certain assimilation between this divinity and the Cretan Zeus may perhaps account for this likeness ; and the discovery of an Egyptian bronze statuette of Amen, another foreign analogue to the indigenous Cretan God, amidst the votive figures

Fig. 15.—Mycenaean Figurine of Bronze from Cave of Hermês Kranaios, near Sybrita, Crete.

---

[1] Both are in the Ashmolean Museum at Oxford.

[2] For specimens of these Syrian bronzes see Perrot, &c., iii. p. 405, No. 277. Helbig, *Question Mycénéenne*, p. 15 seqq. Fig. 6 9. One is from Antaradus (Tartûs), another from Laodicea (Latakieh), and two others from Northern Phoenicia. Another fine ' Hittite' example was in the Tyszkiewicz collection. Helbig, while admitting that the Peloponnesian examples 'révèlent un style

plus souple et qui, par la rondeur de ses formes, se rapprochent déjà considérablement de la nature', regards this as a more recent development of the same Oriental school, and, with Tsuntas ('Εφ. 'Αρχ. 1891, p. 23), sees in them imported ' Phoenician' objects. But the Mycenaean examples are, if anything, earlier in date, and the two groups belong to very different schools, of which the Syrian is (as usual) the more barbarous.

[3] See W. Max Müller, *Asien und Europa*,

of his Cave Sanctuary on Mount Dikta,[1] may not be an altogether fortuitous coincidence.

So many proofs have lately come to hand of the advanced character of Mycenaean civilization that it would certainly be rash to deny the possibility that even in the case of what may be called temple images proper, the transition from the aniconic to the anthropomorphic shape may not already have begun. According to the later Greek tradition[2] sculptors before Daedalos carved images without feet hands or eyes, so that they cannot have been far removed at all events from the simple pillar form. The great step in artistic advance was said to have been made by the mythical craftsman whose activity in the service of Minos seems to represent a real reminiscence of the brilliant creations of Mycenaean art such as we see revealed to us in the Palace of Knossos. The high level thus attained alike in painting and sculpture would seem to be in itself quite compatible with the existence of incipient anthropomorphism in cult images. A small marble hand, more-over, found in the Palace, shows that human figures were at least partially modelled in the round. But there is nothing to prove that the figure in question represented a divinity, and religious conservatism, as well as the great mass of evidence before us, points distinctly the other way.

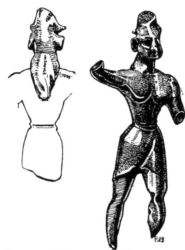

FIG. 16.—MYCENAEAN FIGURINE OF SILVER FROM NEZERO, THESSALY.

It may safely be said that, whatever elements of transition may have made themselves here and there perceptible, the prevailing character of the Mycenaean worship was of the older aniconic kind.

§ 12.—*Illustrative Survivals of Tree and Pillar Cult in Classical Greece and Italy.*

The most obvious and in some respects the most valuable sources of comparison with the Mycenaean cult of trees and pillars are the survivals of this ancient religious stage to be found on the soil of Greece itself. In the most representative cult centres of later Greece indeed, the character of the religious externals had undergone a complete revolution. Palatial temples had succeeded the mere fence or dolmen shrine, the pillar form of the divinity had been developed by successive attempts at anthropomorphism

[1] D. G. Hogarth, *Annual of the British School at Athens*, 1900.

[2] Tzetzes, *Chil.* i. 537. Themistius, *Orationes*, 15. p. 316 a. Cf. Farnell, 'Origins and Earliest Development of Greek Sculpture,' *Archaeological Review*, 1889, p. 169.

into a perfect work of art.[1] Isolated survivals indeed were to be found, such as the stone that represented the Thespian Eros or the wooden column of the Theban Dionysos, but for the most part even the most ancient *xoana* were already half human. The old baetylic and pillar forms, and the sacred trees that overshadowed them, fall into the background to make way for the anthropomorphic image of the divinity. Apollo leans gracefully against the pillar or sits upon the omphalos that were the earlier material representatives of his godhead. What had been already pictorially set forth by the engravers of the Mycenaean signets now belongs to the realities of cult.

Where, as in a few of the most ancient sanctuaries of Greece, the old tree and stone worship still held its own,[2] it is interesting to notice that this phenomenon generally coincides with the survival of the early ethnic stratum that has most claim to represent, in part at least, the Mycenaean element. The Pelasgic Zeus still abode among the oaks of Dodona. Beside the Castalian spring the sacred plane-tree of Zeus Agamemnon and the holy stone of refuge beneath it might claim precedence of the bay and omphalos of the Delphic God. The plane of Helena at Sparta and that of Menelaos at Kaphyae[3] in Arcadia take us back to the same prehistoric stratum of the population. The great Arcadian Zeus, whose only shrine was the oak-woods of Mount Lykaeos, otherwise found his material shape in the twin columns that rose upon its topmost height towards the rising sun, in front of the mound that stood for his altar. The twin pillars, for which we have seen a striking analogy at Knossos[4] in connexion with the Cretan Zeus, had once borne upon them symbolic eagles of the God, indicative of the bird-form under which, according to the widespread primitive belief, a spiritual being descends upon the sacred stone or other object as its possession.[5] So, too, at Tegea, Zeus Teleios was represented by a square image, and Pausanias remarks that the 'Arcadians seem to have an excessive liking for this form.'[6]

In Crete again, where the continuity of early tradition was also exceptionally maintained, the same phenomenon confronts us. This is indeed the classic land of the βαίτυλος, the stone that Kronos swallowed, and which in reality represents the earliest material form of the indigenous Zeus. To the Cretan, too, as to the kindred Carian Zeus in his sanctuary at Labranda, the plane was specially sacred. The planes of Gortyna and of Theren, near Knossos, were celebrated for his union in the one case with Europa, in the other with a Goddess represented as Hera in the later Greek tradition. By Knossos, too, 'near the ruins of the house of Rhea,' was a very

---

[1] On the survival of this aniconic cult in historic Greece and its gradual transformation, see especially, L. R. Farnell, 'The Origins and Earliest Development of Greek Sculpture,' *Archaeological Review*, vol. ii. 1889, p. 167 *seqq.* and his *Cults of the Greek States*, i. p. 13 *seqq.*

[2] For the materials bearing on this subject I need only refer to the exhaustive work of Bötticher, *Der Baumkultus der Hellenen.*

[3] Called Μενελαΐς, Paus. viii. 23, 3.

[4] See below, p. 72.

[5] Paus. viii. 38, 7. M. Bérard, *De l'Origine des Cultes Arcadiens*, p. 73 *seqq.* has rightly seen that the pillars here, like those of the Phoenician Melkarth and other Semitic examples, represent the God. But it is not necessary to accept his conclusion that this shows Phoenician or Semitic influence.

[6] Paus. viii. 48, 6.

ancient holy grove of cypresses,[1] and a black poplar rose before the mouth of
the cave sanctuary of Zeus on Mount Ida. At Gortyna, Phaestos, Aptera,
Hierapytna and other Cretan cities, the tree cult was still sufficiently strong
in classical times to make itself visible on the civic coin-types.

Among the indigenous populations of Italy, the survival of very primitive
forms of tree and stone-worship died hard under later Hellenic influences. It
is probably due to an adoption of local Oenotrian cult that, outside Crete, we
find the best representations of sacred trees, in one case with the sacrificial ox
head hanging from its boughs, on the coin-types of Kaulonia. At Rome itself
nothing can be more complete than the primitive conceptions of stone forms
of divinity, such as Terminus and—to take the most natural interpretation of
the words—Jupiter Lapis, or of tree forms, such as the beech Jupiter Fagutalis,
and the oak Feretrius, from whose branches the *spolia opima* were suspended.
To the Ruminal Fig-Tree there will be occasion to return, nor with Dr.
Frazer's 'Golden Bough' before us need we linger in the Arician Grove. In
later times it was rather in the rustic cult that the full spirit of the primitive
'tree and pillar worship,' continued to assert itself on Italian soil. A rich
storehouse of illustrations is to be found in Greco-Roman reliefs, and especially in the wall-paintings of Pompeii, where we may venture to detect,
beneath the Hellenistic embellishments, something of the old Oscan tradition.
Some of these scenes afford very close comparisons to those that we find represented on the Mycenaean signets. We see the sacred tree surrounded by its
ring fence, or thrusting its branches through its gate-like *sacellum*. Beneath
it still rises the aniconic pillar form of the divinity though here often used
merely as the base of a small image of a sylvan God, or the support of a vase of
offerings. Beneath it, too, is the rustic altar, and from its branches hang the
votive clappers and festoons, and at times the heads of victims. It is interesting to note that, as in prehistoric days, so in later Greco-Roman times
similar scenes of rustic cult are frequent subjects of the intaglios worn in
finger-rings. It may here suffice to cite a single example of such a scene,
engraved on a cornelian found at Rome and belonging to the Imperial
period, which represents a group of three country-people setting up what
appears to be an aniconic *xoanon* or pillar on a square base beneath a sacred
tree.[2]

§ 13.—*The Ficus Ruminalis.*

There can be little doubt that on Greek soil many examples of tree and
pillar worship that are met with in classical times may be regarded as local
survivals of the Mycenaean cult. The early ethnic elements, Pelasgian and
Achaean, with which they are connected, the associations with the House of
Pelops and the Minyans, all point to an unbroken tradition. In Italy, on the
other hand, the survivals of the primitive cult can hardly as a rule claim such

---

[1] Diod. v. 66.

[2] Furtwängler, *Antike Gemmen*, Pl. L. 33. The gem is in my own collection.

a direct relationship. But there is nevertheless some interesting evidence of a cumulative nature, which shows that Rome herself was indebted to prehistoric Greece for some of the oldest elements of her religion.

There can be no reasonable doubt that the *ancilia* represent the Mycenaean form of shield, which has, as we have seen, a profound significance in relation to the cult of the Cretan Zeus. But the whole group of legends that cluster about the Ficus Ruminalis take us back to the same primitive religious cycle. The Sacred Fig-Tree in fact is in a very different case from the beech of Fagutalis, the oak of Feretrius, or the cornel of Quirinus, the cult of which may well have been brought with them by the Latin immigrants from the north of the Apennines. The sanctity of the fig-tree belongs essentially to more southern Mediterranean climes. It was, as has been shown above, a sacred tree of the Mycenaean world, and its veneration was preserved to historic times on Laconian and Attic soil. At Rome, too, we find it traditionally connected with the most primitive element of Greece. Hard by the original seat of the *Ficus Ruminalis* on the Palatine was the Cave of Pan, connected with the old Arcadian cult. The fabled suckling of the twins beneath the tree by the she-wolf reproduces a legend of typically Arcadian form, which recurs in Crete, also in an Arcadian connexion. Arcas himself was the son of the solar Zeus Lykaeos, by Kallisto, who is also a she-bear. Kydon the founder of Kydonia, but also claimed by the Tegeans as of Arcadian descent, the son of Hermes or Apollo and Akakallis a daughter of Minos,[1] was suckled by a bitch.[2] Miletos, the mythical founder of the Cretan city of that name, was nursed by wolves, sent him by his divine father, Apollo.[3] The Cretan Zeus himself is suckled by the goat Amaltheia. The annexed design, representing an infant and horned sheep (Fig. 17), on a clay impression from a seal found with the hieroglyphic archives of the Palace at Knossos, may possibly afford a Mycenaean illustration of a similar legend.

FIG. 17.—1NFANT AND HORNED SHEEP FROM CLAY IMPRESSION OF GEM ; PALACE, KNOSSOS (¾).

In the case of the Roman version a further affinity with this primitive religious cycle seems to be indicated by the fact that the twins suckled here by the she-wolf beneath the tree were the offspring of Mars, who here appears in the aspect of a Sun God,[4] his meeting with Rhea Silvia in the cave being accompanied by an eclipse. Mars here, in fact, is Apollo Lykeios, and, like the Cretan Sun God in the case of Miletos, sends his chosen animal to suckle his offspring. His sacred

---

[1] G. Hoeck, *Creta*, i. 149 and 343.
[2] For the coins of Kydonia see *B.M. Cat.* 'Crete.' Pl. VII. ; Svoronos, *Numismatique de la Crète Ancienne*, Pl. IX. 22–26.

[3] Nikandros, in Antoninus Liberalis, 30.
[4] For the great community between Mars and Apollo, see Furtwängler in Roscher's *Lexikon, s. v.* 'Apollo,' pp. 444, 445.

D

shield, as we have already seen, is a derivative of the Mycenaean type borne by the warrior Sun God of prehistoric Greece.[1] The alternative name of his consort, Rhea, is not less significant and takes us back into the same mythic cycle. Here, too, as in Crete and the Peloponnese, the same traditions are associated with an old Arcadian element. Finally, if we have not here the 'tomb of Mars,' we have at least the tomb of his divine son Romulus, the actual monument of which seems to have been his pillar image, the 'niger lapis,' while the lions set on the bases at either side suggest the most typical of Mycenaean sacral schemes.[2] Religious parallelism could no further go. The coincidences of tradition are beyond the scope of accident and concern details which only the latest archaeological discoveries have brought to light.

§ 14.—*Illustrative Value of Semitic Religious Sources.*

In the preceding sections a few illustrative examples have been given of the survival of the primitive religious phase with which we are concerned in the Greek and Roman world. Some of these, such as the worship of the oak of Dodona, of the planes of Zeus Agamemnon or Menelaos, of the twin pillars of Zeus Lykaeos, or the traditional veneration clinging to the tomb of the Apollo of Amyklae or the Cretan Zeus, are of special interest, as showing the unbroken continuance in certain localities of the religion of Mycenaean Greece. On the whole, however, the remains of the primitive form of worship in classical Greece and Italy are too much overlaid and obscured by the later anthropomorphic tendencies to reproduce its vital spirit otherwise than fitfully and inadequately.

To understand the full force and inwardness of the old religion we have still to turn to the conservative East and notably to the Semitic records. It has ever, indeed, been the essential power of the conquering faiths that have proceeded from that side, that continuing to hold to aniconic forms of worship they have never been tempted to sacrifice the awe and dignity of spiritual conceptions to the human beauty of anthropomorphic cult.

In comparing some of the characteristics of the Mycenaean tree and pillar worship' with that revealed to us principally from Semitic sources as having existed on the eastern shores of the Mediterranean, we are certainly struck by a very deep-lying community. This community, indeed, seems in some respects to go beyond the natural parallelism for which a similar stage

---

[1] It is perhaps also worth remarking that, whereas in the *Ficus Ruminalis* Mars is represented by his sacred bird, the *picus* or woodpecker (Cf. *Mon. dell' Inst.* xi. Tav. 3, 1, the Bolsena Mirror, and the gem in Bötticher, *Baumkultus*, &c. Fig. 37), Kedrênos calls the Cretan Zeus 'Πῖκος.'

[2] Mr. Cecil Smith (*Class. Rev.* 1899, p. 87) has noted, in relation to the recent discoveries,
that the 'niger lapis' of Festus represented a black baetylic stone, such as that of the 'Great Mother' brought to Rome from Pessinus. He also aptly compares the lions beside the 'tombstone' of Romulus with those of Rhea-Kybelê. He further suggests that the so-called Tomb of Romulus being a baetylic stone standing in a *bidental* was naturally a '*locus funestus*.'

of religious evolution might naturally account. It is possible that direct Semitic influences may here and there have left their mark, as Egyptian certainly did, on the externals of Mycenaean worship. But in dealing with the phenomena of this very ancient form of cult, the underlying race connexion between the prae-Hellenic population of Greece and its islands and that of a large Anatolian region must also be taken into account. The ethnographic community, which has left its traces in the names of places and persons from Northern Syria to Western Greece, may well have had its counterpart in the survival of certain specialised forms of primitive religious tradition. At a later date, both in Palestine and Cyprus, we have the evidence of a return wave of Aegean occupation which must also have left its impress on the local cult. In Cyprus this is abundantly clear. On the Canaanite coast we seem to have at least one record of such a process in the late survival of the cult of the Cretan Zeus in Philistine Gaza.

The knowledge of the parallel cults of these East Mediterranean shores comes mainly through a Semitic medium and in a Semitised form. But a large part at least belongs only in a geographical sense to the Semitic world. This ancient underlying religious stratum whether in Anatolia or Palestine was itself simply taken over from the older stock. The pure Semite indeed is difficult to find in these regions. His very type has become Armenoid. In Cilicia and Northern Syria he has largely assimilated elements belonging to that old South Anatolian stock of which the Carians and old Cilicians stand out as leading representatives and which was itself linked on by island stepping stones to prehistoric Greece. In Cyprus the Semite partly absorbed Hellenic elements and converted the Apollo of Amyklae into Reshep Mikal. In Mitanni and other Syrian regions he seems to have imposed his language on a race belonging to the same family as the later Georgian group of Caucasian languages. The Amorites have been ethnically grouped with the Libyans. In Philistia and other parts of the coast of Canaan colonizing Aegean peoples were merged in the same Semitic mass. Gaza was 'Minoan' and the eponymus of Askalon was the brother of Tantalos the founder of the Phrygian Royal House. *Takkarian* Dor, in later days at least, traced its origin from Dôros. The prevailing elements in later Phoenician art more and more declare themselves as decadent Mycenaean, and the partial absorption of the intrusive European plantations on that coast may perhaps account for a spirit of maritime enterprise among the men of Tyre and Sidon quite foreign to Semitic tradition.

The undoubted parallelism observable between the tree and pillar cult of the Mycenaean and that of the Semitic world should be always regarded from this broad aspect. Even where, as will be shown, it extends to details it does not necessarily imply a direct borrowing from Semitic sources. Neither is it necessary to presuppose the existence in the Aegean world of a 'proto-Semitic' element in very early times. The coincidences that we find, so far as they are not sufficiently explained by the general resemblance presented by a parallel stage of religious evolution, may be regarded as parallel survivals due to ethnic elements with European affinities which on the east Mediterranean shores largely underlay the Semitic.[1] We must never overlook the fact that the most primitive culture that has come to light in large parts of Western Asia and in all probability the early population that produced it found its continuation on the European side. Similar classes of pottery, a kindred family of primitive sepulchral images, and apparently allied elements of an early pictography extend from Cyprus through Anatolia to the Greek island world, the Danube Valley, and still further afield. The *labrys* as we have seen is common to the Cretan and the Carian God.

But in any case it is the early religion of the Semitic world which affords the most illuminating commentary on what we are able to reconstruct from remaining records of the Mycenaean tree and pillar cult. It is from this side that the clearest light is thrown on the true inwardness of many of the cult scenes exhibited on the signet rings. It is indeed especially from biblical sources that this form of worship receives its grandest illustration. The Epiphanies and Visions of the Divine Presence beneath sacred trees and beside holy stones and pillars are the most familiar means of Old Testament revelation. It was in triple form beneath the terebinth of Mamre and in the burning bush, that Jehovah first declared himself to Abraham and Moses. So too it was beside the stone beneath his father's terebinth at Ophrah that the Angel of the Lord appeared to Gideon ; and Joshua set up his Stone of Witness ' under the great oak that was by the Sanctuary of the Lord at Shechem.' Sometimes the tree is a terebinth or oak, sometimes the cypress, sometimes the tamarisk, sometimes, as in Deborah's case, the palm. Trees and pillars of Canaanitish Gods were overthrown, but others were planted and set up in honour of the Lord.[2] It was only ' graven images ' that were condemned by the conservative precepts of the earlier Israelite cult.

The worship of the sacred stone or pillar known as *Masseba* or *nosb* is very characteristic of Semitic religion. The classical record of this form of worship is supplied by the biblical account of Jacob's dream with the stone for a pillow beneath his head. ' And Jacob rose up early in the morning, and took the stone that he had put under his head and set it up for a pillar, and poured oil on the top of it.'[3] The pouring oil on the stone was a regular part of the ritual in the case of this pillar worship, and the name given by him to the spot, Beth-el—' the house of God,'—in reality attaches to the sacred stone itself, as appears from Jacob's subsequent vow, ' this stone which I have set up for a pillar shall be God's house.'[4] It was in fact a place of indwelling of the

---

[1] It is the more necessary to bear in mind the above considerations that Dr. H. Von Fritze, in his recently published essay, ' Die Mykenischen Goldringe und ihre Bedeutung für das Sacralwesen,' in *Strena Helbigiana*, p. 73 *seqq.* has revived the endeavour to use the religious parallels observable between the Semitic religion and the Mycenaean cult scenes as an evidence of direct derivation from an Oriental source. He regards the Mycenaean

gold rings as ' imports from the East ' (p. 79), and apparently (p. 82 *seqq.*) as of Phoenician fabric. Were it not for the fact that such views are still advanced, it would hardly seem necessary to point out that the rings belong to the same local Aegean school as the gems.

[2] Cf. Bötticher, *Baumkultus*, p. 520.

[3] Genesis, xxviii. 18.

[4] Genesis xxviii. 22.

divinity. 'Bethel,' or parallel Semitic forms of the same word, have, as we have seen,[1] been brought into connexion with *baetylos*, the stone swallowed by Kronos, in other words the sacred stone of the Cretan Zeus. Whether the derivation is philologically correct or not it is certain that the same religious idea is common to both.

Such 'baetylic' stones among the Semitic peoples might be either stationary or portable like the twelve stones carried off by the representatives of the Twelve Tribes from the bed of Jordan which Joshua afterwards set up at Gilgal.[2] Here we have simply the setting up of rude natural stones like the stone at Bethel, which had been declared holy by certain phenomena attaching to it.

But the later Semitic pillars are very frequently of hewn stone in the shape of a cone, truncated obelisk or column, and must therefore be regarded as the artificial equivalent of the rude stone idols that had preceded them. In some cases they may doubtless have been hewn from some sacred rock and thus stand to the more primitive class exactly in the relation in which the sacred pole or stock stands to the tree from which it was cut. But these later pillars seem in most cases to owe their sanctity to the spot on which they were set up, or to some special rite of consecration as well as to their shape or some holy sign carved on them.

The biblical records again and again attest the cult of the *Ashera*,[3] either as a living tree or its substitute the dead post or pole, before which the Canaanite altars were set.[4] The altar, regularly coupled with the *Ashera* in the primitive Canaanite worship, was doubtless often more than a mere table of offerings[5] and was itself in fact a 'bethel.' In the case of the Ambrosial Stones which stood as the twin representatives of the Tyrian Melkart we find artificially shaped pillars of the more developed cult placed beneath the sacred olive tree of the God.[6]

The sacred trees of the Semites are often endued with a singular animistic vitality which takes us back to a very early religious stage. The tree itself has the power to emit oracular sounds and voices. It was the sound as of marching given forth by the tops of the mulberry trees that was to serve as the divine signal to David for his onslaught on the Philistines.[7] Beneath the palm that bore her name Deborah the prophetess gave forth her soothsayings and drew the inspiration of her judgments.[8] The Arabian hero, Moslim Ben 'Ocba, heard the voice of the gharcad tree appointing

---

[1] See above, p. 14.

[2] Joshua, iv. 5-9, 20-23.

[3] Wrongly translated 'grove' in the Authorised Version.

[4] The opinion that this was a Canaanite Goddess called Ashera is, as Robertson Smith (*Religion of the Semites*, pp. 188, 189) has pointed out, not tenable. 'Every altar had its *Ashera*, even such altars as in the popular, pre-prophetic forms of Hebrew religion were dedicated to Jehovah.' (Cf. Deut. xvi. 21.)

[5] See Robertson Smith, *op. cit.* pp. 204, 205.

[6] The olive tree, with the two pillars beneath it, is represented on colonial coins of Tyre of the third century A.D. They bear the legend ΑΜΒΡΟϹΙΕ ΠΕΤΡΕ (Eckhel, *Doctrina Numorum*, iii. 389; Babelon, *Perses Achém.* p. cxciv., Pl. XXXVII. 9, 11, 16). Cf. Pietschmann, *Gesch. der Phönizier*, p. 295.

[7] II. Samuel v. 24.

[8] Judges iv. 4 *seqq.*

him commander.[1] Holy fires play about the branches of such trees, without consuming them, as in the case of 'the burning bush,' the terebinth of Mamre and the sacred olive tree at Tyre.[2] The tree itself was at times endued with a mysterious power of locomotion and the fable of the trees going forth to choose a king[3] may find its origin in a circle of ideas still represented in modern folklore. The Tyrian olive tree came out of the sea like the Ambrosian Stones that it overshadowed. Macbeth's incredulous exclamation :

> ' Who can impress the forest ; bid the tree
> Unfix his earth-bound root ? '[4]

suggests no difficulty to primitive imagination. The saying of Birnam Wood moving to Dunsinane, rationalised in Shakespeare, receives a more literal fulfilment in Caucasia. Hotly pursued by his enemies the Ossete hero, Khetag of Cabarda, fell powerless outside the sacred grove to which he had fled for protection. A voice came from the linden trees, ' To the grove, Khetag, to the grove !' ' I cannot reach it,' he cried ; ' I am quite worn out. let the grove rather come to me.' Thereupon the grove came and covered him from his enemies, and the glade is pointed out to this day from which the trees removed to save their votary.[5]

We are here no longer on Semitic ground, but the Caucasian folk-tale is singularly illustrative of the old ideas touching the spiritual life of sacred trees and groves, and the asylum given by them.

What gives the tree and pillar cult of the Semitic world and its border-land such a special value as an illustration of the distant records of the Mycenaean worship is its long continuous survival. While the aesthetic sense of the Greeks transformed their rude aniconic idols into graceful human shapes and veiled the realities of tree-worship under elegant allegories of metamorphosis, the conservative East maintained the old cult in its pristine severity. The pillar or cone, or mere shapeless block still stood within the sacred grove as the material representative of the divinity. In the famous black stone of Mecca Islam itself has adopted it, and the traditions of prae-Islamic Arabia maintain themselves in the shape of countless lesser Caabas and holy pillars throughout the Mohammedan world. In how un-changed a form this ancient pillar cult of the Semitic races still survives—even upon what was once counted as Hellenic soil—will be seen from a striking illustration given below from personal experience.[6]

In the foregoing pages it has simply been my object to recall some of the characteristic features of the old Semitic cult, many of them very

---

[1] Robertson Smith, *Religion of the Semites,* p. 133, who compares ' the old Hebrew fable of trees that speak and act like human beings.'

[2] *Op. cit.* p. 193.

[3] Judges ix. 8 *seqq.*

[4] *Macbeth,* act iv. sc. 1.

Svashcheniiya roshdi i derevja u Kav-

kazkih narodov. (In *Reports of the Russian Geographical Society,* Caucasian Section, t. v. p. 158 *seqq.*) Khetag is the legendary ancestor of a peculiar dark-haired tribe among the Ossetes whose badge is the lime tree.

[6] See p. 102 *seqq.*

familiar, in order to bring home something of the inner spirit of what once equally existed on the Aegean side. But over and above the more general points of comparison, such as those already indicated, there are correspondences in the details of the Mycenaean cult which make it necessary to bear in mind the fact already insisted on, that what has come down to us on the other side in a Semitised guise may itself be largely due to the former existence on the more Eastern Mediterranean shores of indigenous ethnic elements akin to those of prehistoric Greece. Into these more special points of conformity it is unnecessary to go minutely at this stage. The idea of the dual, triple and multiple representation of the same divinity in columnar or arboreal groups, external features, such as the shape of the altar base or 'the horns of consecration,' the conception of the sacred pillar itself as performing an architectonic function and serving as an actual 'pillar of the house,'—these and other similar points of coincidence in the Semitic and Mycenaean cults may be cited as showing that the parallelism implies a very close inter-connexion and at times, perhaps, even an underlying ethnic community. In some cases, however, these correspondences receive a simple explanation from a common Egyptian influence, which, as will be shown, has left its mark as clearly upon the externals of the primitive Aegean cult as it did on that of Phoenicia and on the monuments of the 'Hittite' religion that are found throughout a large part of Anatolia and Northern Syria.

§ 15.—*The Horns of Consecration.*

The piece of ritual furniture already referred to above, by anticipation, as 'the horns of consecration,'[1] plays a very important part in the Mycenaean cult. It is a kind of impost or base terminating at the two ends in two horn-like excrescences. At times these terminations have the appearance of being actually horns of oxen, but more generally they seem to be a conventional imitation of what must be regarded as unquestionably the original type. This cult object is evidently of a portable nature. Sometimes it is placed on an altar. Upon the remarkable fragment of a steatite pyxis from Knossos[2] it is laid on the top of a large square altar of isodomic masonry. On the summit of the 'dove shrines' from Mycenae it is superimposed in a reduplicated form on what appears to be the more usual altar-block with incurving sides.[3] At other times it rises above the entablature of an archway[4] connected with a sacred tree or on the roof of a shrine. It is frequently set at the foot of sacred trees. On a crystal lentoid from the Idaean cave[5] we see it in its most realistic and horn-like aspect immediately behind an incurved altar in front of a group of three trees. On a gem from Palaeokastro in Eastern Crete[6] it appears at the foot of a palm-tree. On the vase from Old Salamis it is set

---

[1] See p. 9.
[2] See Fig. 3, p. 5.
[3] See Fig. 65, p. 93.
[4] See Figs. 56, 58.
[5] See Fig. 25, p. 44.
[6] See below, p. 56.

at the foot of the double axe or *labrys*, which in this case is less a symbol than a material impersonation of the divinity. It is equally associated with sacred pillars. On a Mycenaean gold ring it is placed at the foot of such a pillar, here seen within a shrine, [1] and it is unquestionably the same ritual object which is outlined beneath the three pillar idols on the dove-shrines from the third Akropolis grave.[2] Its appearance in a reduplicated form on the altar which forms the central prominence above has already been noted, and in addition to this it is also repeated above the entablature of what may be described as the lateral chapels, the doves here using the outermost horns as a perch. It thus appears no less than seven times on each of the gold shrines. In the remarkable fresco painting to be described below of the façade of a small Mycenaean temple from the Palace of Knossos this article of cult appears at the foot of both the two columns of the central shrine, and on either side of each of those in the wings. On another fresco fragment from the same site reproduced in Fig. 18 four pairs of 'horns of consecration' are visible above the wall of what is evidently another sanctuary.

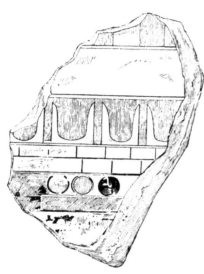

FIG. 18.—HORNS OF CONSECRATION ON SANCTUARY WALL, FROM FRESCO OF PALACE, KNOSSOS.

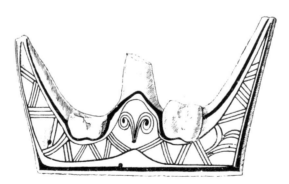

FIG. 19.—HORNED CULT OBJECT OF PAINTED POTTERY: IDAEAN CAVE.

An actual example of a similar article of cult may with great probability be recognised in a hitherto unexplained relic [3] of painted terracotta (Fig. 19)

---

[1] See below p. 92.

[2] See p. 93.

[3] Since this paragraph was written, Dr. P.

Wolters has made the same suggestion (*Jahrbuch d. k. d. Arch. Inst.* 1900, p. 148).

terminating in two horn-like projections found in the Votive Cave at Patso in Crete later dedicated to Hermes Kranaios.[1] A conical stem and two curved objects are seen between the two horns, but the upper part of these is broken off and their signification remains enigmatic. They represented no doubt the sacred object to which the clay horns were dedicated.

In some cult scenes, as we shall see, only a single horn is visible, but its presence probably implies the existence of another. There can be little doubt that in all these cases we have to do with a more or less conventionalised article of ritual furniture derived from the actual horns of the sacrificial oxen. The setting of the horns of the slaughtered animals before the cult image or upon the altar is a very familiar usage of primitive worship.

These Mycenaean ' horns of consecration ' suggest at once the 'horns of the altar ' of Hebrew ritual. These horns were no longer the actual horns of the victims, being of the same wood as the altar itself, in this respect standing to the original in the same secondary and symbolic relation as those of their Mycenaean equivalent. In this case there were four horns, one at each corner and these were of one piece with the altar.[2] But an absolute parallel with the Mycenaean usage on the Semitic side is to be found in a representation on the stele of the God Salm found at Teima in Northern Arabia and now in the Louvre[3] (Fig. 20). The priest of this divinity is there seen before an altar having upon it two horns of consecration with the head of a votive ox immediately above. The cult object is here in a separate piece and corresponds both in form and position to its Mycenaean counterpart, as seen for instance on the altar of the Knossian pyxis.

Fig. 20.—Altar with Horned Cult Object above, from Stele of God Salm.

No parallel could be more complete.

A later illustration of a usage analogous to the placing of the ' horns of consecration' before the baetylic idol is to be found on a coin struck at Byblos under the Emperor Macrinus (Fig. 21),[4] representing the temple of the local

---

[1] F. Halbherr e P. Orsi, *Antichità dell' Antro di Zeus Ideo*, Tav. XIV. 3 and p. 227. Part of the horn of another similar object was found. Both were presented by Mr. T. A. Triphylli to the Museum of the Syllogos at Candia, together with other votive objects of Mycenaean date from the same cave.

[2] Exodus xxvii. 2.

[3] Perrot et Chipiez, *L'Art*, &c. t. iv. p. 392, Fig. 206, from which the above sketch is taken.

[4] The figure in the text has been specially drawn from a specimen of the coin in the British Museum. For other examples see

Astarte. In the centre of the court is seen the aniconic image of the Syrian Goddess in the form of a cone the base of which is enclosed by what appears to be a square lattice-work fence. The front side of this screen, which is all that is visible, shows two hornlike projections rising at each end. As there was probably one at each corner this arrangement shows a great resemblance to the 'horns of the altar' of biblical usage.

§ 16.—*Trinities and other Groups of Trees and Pillars.*

A noteworthy feature in the Semitic versions of the pillar cult is the setting up of more than one aniconic image of the divinity at the same spot.

FIG. 21.—CONE OF ASTARTE IN HORNED ENCLOSURE, TEMPLE COURT, BYBLOS, ON COIN OF MACRINUS (?)

At an earlier stage this is well illustrated by the twelve stones of Gilgal; at a later period by the votive stelae of Carthage and of Northern Arabia. On the Carthaginian stelae it is not infrequent to see three divine pillars like truncated obelisks, grouped together within the same shrine and upon a single base. In Fig. 22, from Nora (Capo di Pula) in Sardinia,[1] the symbol

---

Donaldson, *Architectura Numismatica*, No. 20. P. et C. iii. p. 60, Fig. 19; Pietschmann, *Geschichte der Phönizier*, pp. 200, 201.

[1] Copied by me in the Museum at Cagliari, where are several votive stones of the same kind from Capo di Pula. In other cases there are two *stelae* on the same base. On a votive monument from Hadrumetum (Susa) (Pietsch-

above the central stele seems to mark the presence of Tanit, here represented in a triple form. On a votive monument from Lilybaeum bearing a dedication to Baal Hammon a worshipper stands before an incense altar accompanied by the symbol of divinity and a caduceus, while above is a base with three pillars of the usual kind.[1] Here again the trinity of pillars is still the abode of a single divinity, in this case Baal Hammon. Elsewhere we see two groups of three pillars and the divine symbols above them, and on a monument from Hadrumetum as many as nine pillars in a triple group of three occur on a single base.[2]

In the votive niches of the ancient sanctuary discovered by Doughty at Medáin Sâlih in north-western Arabia the aniconic form of a single

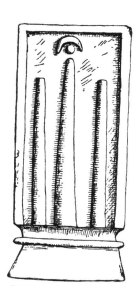

FIG. 22.—CARTHAGINIAN PILLAR SHRINE ON STELE, NORA, SARDINIA.

FIG. 23.—GROUP OF SACRED PILLARS ON MYCENAEAN VASE FROM HALIKI.

divinity is found indifferently represented by a single pillar or by groups of two or three.[3] One of the niches, in this case containing a single

mann, *Geschichte der Phönizier*, p. 205) a single broad base, of the same form as that of Fig. 22, supports two smaller bases, with separate panels, each bearing a triple group of pillars. Above one panel is the orb and crescent; above the other the Carthaginian sign of divinity, a development of the Egyptian *Ankh* or life symbol.

[1] *Corpus. Inscrip. Semit.* i. 1. No. 138 ; P. Berger, *Rev. Arch.* 3rd s. iii. pp. 209–214 ;

P. et C. iii. p. 308, Fig. 232 ; cf. Pietschmann, *op. cit.* p. 206.

[2] Pietschmann, *op. cit.* p. 205.

[3] See Doughty, *Travels in Arabia Deserta*, i. p. 121 and p. 187 ; *Documents Épigraphiques recueillis dans le Nord de l'Arabie*, pp. 21–23, Pl. XLV. XLVI. ; Ph. Berger, *L'Arabie avant Mahomet d'après les Inscriptions*, 1885, p. 19 ; P. et C. iv. p. 389–391.

pillar, bears a Nabataean inscription proclaiming the rock-shrine to be the Mesgeda (or Mosque) of 'Aouda the great God of Bostra' who seems elsewhere, like Baal Hammon and Tanit, to be represented in a dual or triple form.

It thus appears that throughout the Semitic world a single spiritual being could infuse itself at one and the same time into several material abodes. Groups of two or three pillars could be the visible embodiment of a single divinity—a conception which readily lent itself to such mystic dogmas as that of a triune God or Goddess, applied in the above instances to Baal and Tanit. It may be observed that the primitive conceptions underlying the adoration of the Cross have much in common with this Semitic pillar worship, and the Armenians to this day set up groups of three crosses, into which the Spirit of the Trinity in Unity is called upon to enter by a solemn rite of consecration.[1]

I venture to believe that a group of divine pillars, closely analogous to those of the Carthaginian stelae and North Arabian shrines, may be recognised in the design on a Mycenaean painted vase from Haliki near Athens[2] (Fig. 23). The central object here seems to be a somewhat conventionalised rendering of a volute column, above which is a kind of triple halo, which may be compared with the radiate emanations of the Cypriote pillars.[3] On either side of this central column are two pairs of smaller pillars in decreasing order, above each of which is a disc with a central dot identical with the Egyptian solar symbol. We recall the orb and crescent placed in a similar position above the Carthaginian pillar idols.

An analogous Mycenaean example of a group of sacred pillars is supplied by a recently discovered lentoid intaglio from Mycenae, in which a male figure is seen in the act of adoration before five columns of architectural character with vertical and spiral flutings. (Fig. 24.)

It is perhaps worth considering whether the well-known dove shrines of Mycenae may not supply a parallel of another kind to the religious conception of more than one aniconic pillar representing the same divinity. These shrines present three openings, in each of which is a similar column, the divine character of which is attested by the appearance at its base of the Mycenaean 'horns of consecration.'[4] It is to be noted that above the shrines is only a

---

[1] I am informed of this usage by my friend Mr. F. C. Conybeare. The special consecration in the case of the Armenian crosses is partly due to the necessity of previously exorcising the evil spirits inherent in the material substance of the crosses.

[2] Furtwängler und Löschke, *Mykenische Vasen*, p. 39, Fig. 23. Few, I imagine, will agree with Dr. Ohnefalsch-Richter's view (*Kypros die Bibel und Homer*, p. 112), that we have here fantastic representations of wooden poles 'with human heads,' the middle one wearing a crown.

[3] See below, p. 51.

[4] I observe that Dr. Ohnefalsch-Richter (*Kypros die Bibel und Homer*, p. 183), though he has not understood the object of the foot of the columns, has rightly recognised in them Mycenaean *Massebas*, and compared their triple form with the Semitic groups. He saw in them 'Drei Chammanim . . . die Abgessandten der Androgynen Gottheit Moloch-Astarte.' It is hardly necessary to observe that this precise attribution, and indeed the whole supposition, that they are purely and simply Semitic pillar idols, goes far beyond the evidence at our disposal.

single altar, so that if we have not here a single divinity in a triple form we have at least to do with σύνβωμοι. The doves certainly recall the Carthaginian and Libyan shrines of Tanit, whose pillar idol is so often three times repeated—in that case, however, in a single shrine.

The trimorphic or triune conception of divinity seems to represent a very early element in Greek religion, of which many survivals, such as the triple Hekate, may be noted in later times. The most interesting of these survivals is to be found in the later cult of Minyan Orchomenos, where, down to Pausanias's time, the images of the Graces, which were contained in the most ancient sanctuary of the place and received the greatest veneration, were three natural stones, which were said to have fallen from heaven. It was only in his own time that this group of primitive baetylic pillars was supplemented by artistically carved images.[1]

On one of the more recently discovered gold signets from Mycenae[2] appears a sacral doorway, which at first sight seems to offer a more

FIG. 24.—WORSHIP OF GROUP OF PILLARS ON CYLINDER, MYCENAE (¾)

literal parallel than any of the above to the threefold groups of baetylic pillars on votive or Carthaginian stelae and Arabian cave 'mosques.' Three apparent columns are seen ranged together within its open portal, but closer inspection shows that they are in fact the trunks of a group of three trees, whose branches rise above the impost of the shrine, which is thus shown to be of the hypaethral class. This triplet of sacred trees recurs on other Mycenaean seals, and may with great probability be regarded as the cult equivalent of the trinity of pillars in the dove shrines.

A good example of the worship of a trinity of sacred trees is supplied by a rock crystal lentoid found in the Idaean Cave,[3] (Fig. 25). Here a female votary is seen blowing a conch-shell or triton before an altar of the usual Mycenaean shape. Above the altar is seen a group of three trees apparently cypresses, and immediately in front of them the 'horns of con-

---

[1] Paus. ix. 38, 1.
[2] See below p. 85.
[3] L. Mariani, 'Antichità Cretesi' (*Mon. Ant.* vi. 1895, p. 178, Fig. 12); Furtw. *Ant. Gemm.* iii. p. 47, Fig. 22. Fig. 25 represents an enlarged drawing by Mr. F. Anderson from a cast obtained by me some years since at Candia. The gem is in the Museum of that town.

secration.' To the right of the altar is a rayed symbol, to the left is apparently another altar base, with a conical excrescence, and behind the votary another tree. From this gem it appears that the conch-shell trumpet performed a ritual function in summoning the divinity. It may be observed that triton shells have been found in the Mycenaean bee-hive tombs in Crete, and are still in common use in the island, especially among the village guards (χωροφύλακες), as a means of raising an alarm or calling for help.

FIG. 25.—WORSHIP OF GROUP OF TREES: CRYSTAL LENTOID, IDAEAN CAVE.

A triple group of trees, with their trunks closely drawn together, and having indeed the appearance of a single tree with a tripartite trunk, is presented by the gold signet ring from Mycenae, for the first time published in Fig. 56 below.[1]

It is noteworthy that the sacred tree beneath which the Goddess is seated on the great gold ring from the Akropolis Treasure of Mycenae, exhibits the same tripartite stem.[2]

The equation of sacred tree and pillar makes it equally natural for the divinity to find a multiple impersonation in the arboreal as the stony shape. Of this too parallels are abundant on Semitic ground. The divinity may have a grove or group of trees as a place for indwelling, as well as a single tree. On a Babylonian cylinder,[3] a pair of trees rises behind a God apparently defined as Sin by a crescent symbol. The fact that when Jehovah first revealed Himself to Abraham beneath ' the terebinths of Mamre,' He took the form of three persons, seems to point to the conclusion that there was here a special group of three holy trees.

In Egyptian cult, which in some of its most ancient elements shows a deep affinity with that of the Semitic world, we find evidences of groups of trees representing a single divinity. The god Min, whose worship, as is shown by the remains of his Koptos sanctuary, goes back into pre-historic times, is seen with two,[4] three,[5] or five [6] cypresses, representing his arboreal

---

[1] See p. 84.
[2] See Fig. 4, p. 10.
[3] Lajard, *Culte de Mithra,* xxvii. 6 ; *Culte du Cyprès,* ix. 3.
[4] Wilkinson, *Manners and Customs of the Ancient Egyptians* (1878 ed.), iii. p. 24, Fig. 504.
[5] On a stele excavated by Prof. Petrie at Koptos, now in the Ashmolean Museum.

Fig. 26 is taken from a drawing of this kindly made for me by Mr. C. F. Bell.

[6] Wilkinson, *op. cit.* i. p. 404, Fig. 173, iii. Pl. LX. E. ; Rosellini, *Monumenti dell' Egitto,* iii. LVI. 3, and cf. Ohnefalsch-Richter, *Kypros,* &c. Taf. cliii. 1, and p. 461, who compares the votive cypresses of the Cypriote sanctuaries.

shape placed behind him, either on a small shrine, on a base resembling a series of doorways (Fig. 26), or on a stand, the upper part of which has the characteristic moulding of an Egyptian house or shrine.   In one case a king stands in front of the God, offering two miniature models of the same tree.   At times the stand or shrine supporting the group of trees is carried by priests, like the Ark of the Covenant.[1]   It will be seen that an Egyptian stand, similar to that which supports the tree equivalents of Min, served as the prototype of the bases on which are placed the baetylic pillars of the Carthaginian cult (see Fig. 22).   On the same stelae, and again on the Cypro-Phoenician bowls,[2] it also serves as a pedestal for figures of the Gods themselves.   It is true that Egyptian bases and stands with this characteristic profile and square moulding were also of more general usage,[3] but the application of this form of support, in the one case for the sacred trees, in the other for the pillar idols, and again for the divinities themselves, is at least a suggestive coincidence.

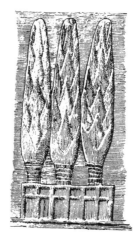

Fig 26.—Tree Trinity. of Min.

It is interesting to note that the alternative appearance of the tree impersonation of the God Min above either a shrine or a sacral base presents the closest parallels to the Mycenaean types in which the trees are placed immediately above the altar as in Fig. 25, or behind a sacred doorway as in Fig. 57.   On the other hand the superposition of the Semitic and Libyan sacred pillars on the Egyptian base shows a perfect analogy with the placing of the column on the Mycenaean base or altar-block in the Lions' Gate scheme.

§ 17.—'The Pillar of the House.'

Another feature in the Aegean cult of baetylic pillars which finds a close analogy in the Semitic world is not only the frequent appearance of such pillars in an architectonic form, but their actual performance of a structural function   A very ancient parallel to such a usage may also be found in the Hathoric columns of Egyptian temples and, in another form, in the sacred Dad or Tat pillar with its fourfold capital that was supposed to support the four quarters of the heavens.   In the Lions' Gate at Mycenae, and still more in the sacred columns of the small temple of which a wall-

---

[1] Wilkinson, *op. cit.* iii. Pl. LX. E.

[2] On the patera of Amathus, for instance (P. and C. iii. p. 774, Fig. 547), bases of this type serve as pedestals for hawk-headed divinities, and for the scarabaeus that they adore.

[3] *E.g.* as a table (Wilkinson, *Manners and Customs of the Ancient Egyptians*, i. p. 418, Fig. 194, 2); as the plinth of a building (*op. cit.* i. p. 346, Fig. 114, 1).

painting has been preserved in the Palace of Knossos,[1] will be found illustrations of the same religious idea. In a succeeding section we shall see
the stone supports of the more primitive dolmen shrines of Mycenae already
performing functions at at once the aniconic habitation of divinity and

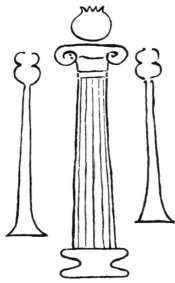

FIG. 27.—SACRED COLUMN ON
STELE, CARTHAGE.

pillars of the house' and there will be occasion to point out some near parallels among
the early megalithic structures of the
Balearic and Maltese islands.

Many of the baetylic pillars of Semitic
cult can be shown to have had the same
architectonic form or even to have performed
structural functions as supporting the architrave of a building. We are indeed ex-
pressly told of the brazen pillars set up by
Solomon at the porch of the Temple that
they were provided with capitals adorned
with a network of pomegranates and of
" lily " shape[2]. In the same way Solomon's
friend and contemporary, Hiram of Tyre, is
recorded to have set up a golden column in
the temple of Baal.[3] Free-standing columnar impersonations of the deity often
supporting pomegranates are frequent on
Carthaginian stelae [4] (Fig. 27). At times
the divine character of these is marked by a
bust of Tanit placed upon the capital,[5] or
her globe and crescent symbol appears upon the shaft. Tyrian [6] and Cypro-
Phoenician [7] columns of the same class show the same symbols—here connected
with Istar—carved upon capitals derived from the Egyptian lotus-type,
a parallel which recalls Jakim and Boaz.

The names of the two columns in the front of Solomon's temple—' the
Stablisher,' and 'in Him is Strength,' which show that they were there placed as
symbolic forms of Jehovah,[8] would derive additional force if we might believe

---

[1] See below, p. 94 *seqq*.

[2] 1 Kings vii. 15 *seqq.* ; cf. Jeremiah li. 21
seqq. The Capitals are described as of ' Lily
Work' (1 Kings vii. 19). An elaborate
restoration of these columns has been made
by Chipiez (P. and C. t. iv. Pl. VI. and cf. p.
314 *seqq.*). But the lotus form is better given
by De Vogüé, *Le Temple*, Pl. XIV.

[3] Menander of Tyre, cited by Josephus,
Antiq. viii. 5. It is called the temple of
' Zeus.'

[4] Copied by me in the Museum of Carthage.
Cf. P. et C. t. iv. Fig. 167, p. 324, Fig. 168,
p. 325.

[5] *Gazette Archéologique*, iv. 1884 Pietschmann, *Geschichte der Phönizier*, p. 210.
(Votive stone from Hadrumetum.)

[6] In the Louvre, Musée Napoléon III.
Pietschmann, *op. cit.* p. 274.

[7] Three in the Louvre are given in P. et C.
iii. p. 116, Figs. 51, 52, 53. Cf Pietschmann,
op. cit. p. 277. Four more capitals of the same
kind, from votive stelae in the sanctuary of
Aphroditê at Idalion, are figured by Ohnefalsch-Richter, *Kypros, die Bibel und Homer*,
Taf. lviii. lix.

[8] Cf. Robertson Smith, *Religion of the
Semites*, p. 208, *n*. 1.

that they actually performed a structural function in supporting the roof beams of the porch.[1] The duality of the columns in this case as in that of the bronze pillars of Melkart, in the sanctuary at Gades, at least points to the possibility of their having served a purpose of this kind, and the twin columnar forms of the divinity on either side of some of the Carthaginian shrines actually support an entablature.[2] By the 'two pillars of the house' of Dagon, which Samson is said to have overthrown at Gaza, are probably meant the pillars of the porch from the roof of which the Philistine lords would have watched the sport provided for them by the blinded hero. But the above analogies suggest that they may have actually represented the dual columnar form of Dagon himself, and though this feature in the story is not brought out by the narrator, it would certainly add a special point to the exploit.

Whether or not the two columns of Solomon's porch, or those of Melkart's temple actually themselves performed structural functions, it is certain that these Semitic types of the divine pillar were based on architectural models. Their columnar shape represents the divinity as 'a pillar of the house.' In the case of the Mycenaean examples of the same class their origin from wooden columns is clearly indicated by the round ends of the cross beams above the entablature as shown on the Lions' Gate and elsewhere. But this leads us to the obvious explanation as to at least one way in which the actual supporting pillars of a building could be regarded as having themselves a divine character. It would appear that the indwelling might of a tutelary God was secured by using in the principal supports of important buildings the wood of sacred trees. On the Mycenaean signets we shall see the columnar idol alternating in a similar position between the heraldic guardians, such as sphinxes and griffins, with the sacred tree.[3] A curious instance is recorded of an unsuccessful attempt to convert a sacred tree to similar usage for a Christian temple. A wonder-working cedar, that had been transported from Lebanon to the King's garden at Mtsket, was cut down by King Miriam, to be used in the construction of the church, which he there founded. But in spite of all their efforts the workmen were unable to set up the trunk that was to support the roof. St. Nin then prayed for the scattering of the evil spirits, and in the night a youth with a fiery garment was seen to carry back the trunk to the height on which the tree had stood, and set it on its roots, whereupon it grew together again, and sweet-scented myrrh oozed forth from it as of old. It was only later that bishop John seeing the miraculous cures worked by the tree, and the idolatrous worship offered to it, made a more successful effort at its conversion, and with the aid of a hundred men brought it down once more and hewed it into a cross, in which shape it prolonged its wonder-working powers.[4] A conspicuous instance of the employment of the

---

[1] The free-standing pillars shown outside the temple of Paphos on either side of the central opening with the cone of Aphroditê have been brought into comparison with Jakim and Boaz. They are sometimes however incense altars.

[2] Cf. a Carthaginian stela from Sulcis in Sardinia. P. et C. iii. p. 253, Fig. 193. The entablature bears the winged disk and uraei.

[3] Compare below, p. 57 *seqq.*

[4] ' Svashcheniiya roshdi i derevja u Kavkazkih narodov,' *op. cit.* t. v. (Tiflis, 1877-1878).

E

trunk of a sacred tree as a 'pillar of the house' is afforded by a Byblian legend preserved by Plutarch.[1] The divine tamarisk, whose trunk had grown about the chest of Osiris, was cut down by the King 'Malkandros,' of Byblos the husband of 'Queen Astarte,' who had been amazed at its size, and made the principal support of his roof,[2]—in other words it was 'the pillar of the house' of Melkart. Removed at Isis' request to enable her to cut out the concealed chest of Osiris, the rest of the wooden pillar was transferred to the temple of Isis at Byblos, where it was still an object of worship in Plutarch's day. At Byblos it must be borne in mind that Isis and Osiris in reality represent Astarte and Adonis.[3]

In all this we see the columnar idol of the architectonic type taking its rise in the most natural way from the hewn trunk of a sacred tree made use of as 'a pillar of the house,' with the object of securing the presence of the divine 'Stablisher' inherent in the material. The character of the columnar divinity being thus fixed by its structural function in a wooden building can be taken over into stone or metal work, the conventional shape as in the case of Christian crosses supplying here the consecration no longer inherent in the material itself. In this secondary stage, however, the sanctity of such tutelary columns is generally further marked as at Tyre, Carthage and in the Phoenician remains of Cyprus by the addition of some symbol of divinity such as the orb and crescent, or as both on Semitic soil and at Mycenae by the coupling with it of its sacred animals.

§ 18.—*Egyptian Influences, and the Rayed Pillars of Mycenaean Cyprus.*

The extreme antiquity of the anthropomorphic and here often zoomorphic form of cult image in Egypt may make it at first seem unprofitable to look for illustrations of the primitive aniconic cult of the Greek and Semitic world on that side. As a matter of fact, nevertheless, the old religious moment has left clear records in Egyptian monuments. The pre-historic figures of the god Min, discovered by Mr. Flinders Petrie at Koptos, still largely partake of the pillar form, and his equivalent materialisation, as a group of trees, survived through the historic period. The obelisk of the Sun-God Ra again represents the survival of the old cult image in a more artificial form. In the pillars with the head of Hathor we see a compromise between the aniconic and anthropomorphic type, frequent in later Greek religion, and the actual employment of these divine columns as supports of temples has been shown to have a very interesting bearing on a characteristic feature of the Mycenaean and the Semitic pillar cult.[4] The Dad or Tat pillar (once called the Nilometer) with its quadruple capital indicative of the four supports of heaven, also at times becomes partially anthropomorphised like the Hathoric columns.

---

[1] *De Iside et Osiride*, c. 15, 16. Isis hovers round the pillar in the form of a swallow.

[2] C. 15, ἔρεισμα τῆς στέγης; c. 16, τὴν κίονα τῆς στέγης.

[3] Robertson-Smith, *op. cit.* p. 191.

[4] See above, p. 45.

The vegetable columns of Egypt, such as those derived from forms of the lotus and blue water-lily, are also in their nature sacred. Closely connected with these is a type of floral capital, the general outline of which, with its recurved side petals, may be often compared to a fleur-de-lys, the upper leaf of which is, however, generally provided with a marginal outgrowth of fan-like sprays so as to resemble a palmette. Two theories have been put forward to explain the origin of this palmette pillar. According to one version [1] it is simply due to an otherwise substantiated pictorial convention, first pointed out by Dr. Borchardt, in which the Egyptian artist combined the inside and profile view of an object. In this view the palmette and its side sprays represent half of the circle of a lotus flower as seen from above, with its radiating petals superimposed on the calix as seen in profile. Dr. Borchardt himself, on the other hand, points to the columns surmounted by fourfold capitals, among which this occurs, together with the lotus, the blue water-lily and the papyrus, as showing by analogy that it represents a distinct species. He calls it a 'lily' capital,[2] but there can be little doubt that the real original is the iris, which in our heraldic fleur-de-lys gave birth to a very parallel development on European soil. A similar evolution to a pure palmette form took place in Persia, where the iris is a favourite artistic motive. Several features in the flower itself combine towards this decorative evolution. The veining of the petals with a central stem from which minor striations radiate, their crinkled edges and the frequent association of the central upright petal, with two smaller seen edgewise on either side, are all so many elements which contribute in one way or another to suggest the idea of a palmette, already familiar in the East. But some iris types exhibit features which make the comparison with the palmette even more obvious. The beautiful *Iris reticulata* of the East Mediterranean countries has smaller petals growing out of the central vein of the larger in a fan-like fashion. The recurved ends of the lower petals again produce a decorative effect in Persian art, and in some types of the heraldic fleur-de-lys, closely resembling the drop-like excrescence on many of the Egyptian palmette pillars, which have puzzled archaeologists. They have been explained as drops of water in the act of falling from freshly emerged lotus flowers. But the idea is forced and the flower is not a lotus.

These palmette capitals are not apparently found in Egyptian art earlier than the eighteenth Dynasty, and they now seem to supersede the simple lily-like flower of Upper Egypt, which perhaps represents a flowering rush. Is it possible that this change in Egyptian decorative fashion was due to Mycenaean

---

[1] Flinders Petrie, *Egyptian Decorative Art*, pp. 68, 69.

[2] L. Borchardt, *Die Ægyptische Pflanzensäule*, p. 18 *seqq.*; *Die 'Lilien'säulen.* In the Old and Middle Kingdom a simple 'lily' type appears. It is only from the time of the Eighteenth Dynasty, however, that the type appears described by Borchardt as 'the lily with pendants,' and above as the iris or fleur-de-lys.

influence,[1] as to the strength of which the monuments of Tell-el-Amarna afford such remarkable evidence ?   The holy character of the iris on Hellenic soil is bound up, as is well known, with the legends of one of the most ancient indigenous divinities, Apollo Hyakinthos.[2]   It seems, however, to have escaped notice that of the two kinds of flowers, evidently bearing a sacred character, offered by an attendant votary to the seated Goddess on the great signet ring from Mycenae,[3] one is a lily, the other an iris, which, moreover, shows the characteristic palmette development.   In a religious scene which, as will be shown, refers to the consort of an armed solar divinity, the appearance of this ancient emblem of Hyakinthos is not, perhaps, without significance.

Whether or not, however, we are to recognise in the appearance of the palmette capital on eighteenth Dynasty monuments an Egyptian adaptation of a Mycenaean religious motive, the essential fact with which we have to deal is that this fleur-de-lys type now takes its place beside the sacred lotus.

These palmette, or iris, columns, often provided with fantastic side sprays, form a common device of the glazed rings and moulds for such found in the Palace of Tell-el-Amarna.[4]   The incurving side sprays, seen on many of these composite vegetable forms, often recall those that rest on either side of the head-piece—the house of Horus—on the head of the Goddess Hathor. Closely allied, moreover, to this symbolic group are actual Hathoric posts or pillars with uraei curving up on either side of their base.[5]

These palmette pillars, and the more fantastic symbolic attachments into which they merge, have a great interest in their bearing on a whole series of derivative designs on a class of cylinders to which the name Cypro-Mycenaean can be appropriately given.   These religious types, which are characteristic of the period of Mycenaean colonisation in Cyprus, belong to a separate category from the Aegean class, and form the subject of a special study of which it is only necessary here to reproduce a few summary results.

The Cypro-Mycenaean cylinder types unfold a series of religious scenes in which the central object appears in three inter-related forms.

It may be described thus :—

> (a) A palmette column ;
> (b) A fantastic vegetable pillar with a rayed summit ;
> (c) A rayed pillar or obelisk.

---

[1] This is Mr. F. Ll. Griffith's suggestion. He considers that the adoption of the iris type in eighteenth dynasty times may be due to Mycenaean influence.

[2] The literature regarding the flower ὑάκινθος has been summarised by Greve (Roscher's *Lexikon*, s. v. ' Hyakinthos.') The conclusion is 'es ist jedenfalls eine Irisart aber unbestimmt welche.'

[3] Fig. 4, p. 10.

[4] Petrie, *Tell-el-Amarna*, 199 *seqq*. Similar designs are seen on the moulds for glazed wall flowers from the same site, Pl. XVIII. 369 *seqq*. At times these are crossed with elements taken from the lotus.

[5] See below, p. 52.

Examples of the two former classes are given on Fig. 28, 4–7, and the dependence of the two first on the contemporary Egyptian prototypes, illustrated in the same figure (Nos. 1–3), becomes self evident. The rays of the Cypriote pillar are, in fact, directly suggested by the radiating leaflets of the palmette type.

But the radiation itself, though its pictorial representation was thus facilitated by certain features in the symbolic Egyptian pillar, has also a distinct religious value. The rays indeed as the natural concomitant of divinities of light are a very ancient oriental tradition. Samas the Babylonian Sun-God is habitually represented with rays issuing from his shoulders and radiate divinities of the same class are not infrequent in the neighbouring Syrian and Anatolian regions[1] which show a certain analogy with these Cypro-Mycenaean pillars. The luminous baetylic pillars of Melkart at Tyre repeat the same idea. How natural even to savage races is the addition of rays to the rude image that represents the Sun Spirit is well illustrated by a religious usage of the modern Melanesians. In the New Hebrides the stone which is regarded as the potential dwelling-place of the Sun Spirit ' is laid upon the ground and a circle of white rods which stand for sunbeams are set round so as to radiate from it in all directions.' [2]

FIG. 28.—EGYPTIAN PALMETTE PILLARS AND
THE RAYED PILLARS OF CYPRUS.
1—3. Egyptian Pillars. 4—7. Cypro-Mycenaean
Derivatives.

In the radiation of the Cypriote pillars we see an adaptation of the radiating leaflets on the original palmette to a very widespread and primitive idea connected with solar pillars and images. The monsters associated with these columns as guardians and adorants are quite in keeping with this solar attribution. The griffins, sphinxes and lions that we see here before the sacred pillar or pillar tree are all taken from the Egyptian solar cycle. Of the Hathoric sprays attached to some of the more fantastic columns we have already spoken. In several cases, however, an adapted version of Hathor herself appears in long robes with a cow's head, and on one cylinder this figure is followed by a griffin adorant whose head is surmounted by the head-piece of the Goddess, the house of Horus, between two incurving sprays. On the important bearing of these designs on the cult of Mycenaean Cyprus this

[1] See especially Pietschmann, *Geschichte der Phönizier*, p. 225, who gives a good example of a rayed divinity with a pillar-shaped body, from the marble basin found at Sidon, now in the Berlin Museum. He compares with this certain representations of divinities on the coins of Demetrios II., Nikator (P. Gardner, *B.M.Cat.* 'Seleucid Kings of Syria,' Pl. XVIII. 1, and XXV. 2), and others struck under Antoninus Pius in the Cilician town of Mallos.

[2] R. H. Codrington, *The Melanesians* p. 184.

is not the place to enlarge. It may be sufficient to observe that in this period of Cypriote history the "golden Aphroditê" of the Egyptians seems to play a much more important part than any form of Astarte or Mylitta.

These Cypriote examples are of special interest in their bearing on certain religious types and associations from the Aegean area of the Mycenaean world. The more specialised forms of the rayed, fantastic, tree pillar are peculiar to Cyprus, but even these find analogies in some hitherto unexplained figures on Mycenaean vases, and we shall also see rayed divinities. On the other hand a simple form of the palmette pillar, approaching a fleur-de-lys in outline, is found on Mycenaean signets and the same group of guardian monsters recur in association with a whole series of Mycenaean pillars. The Cypriote parallels will be found to have a fundamental importance as demonstrating in detail that these are in fact taken over from the cult of Mentu-Ra the Warrior Sun-God of Egypt, of Hathor, and of Horus.

It is reasonable to believe that in the Aegean area as well as in Cyprus this taking over of the external elements from the Egyptian solar cycle was facilitated by underlying resemblances in the characters of the indigenous divinities to whom these attributes were transferred. The surviving attachment of some of these solar monsters to certain later divinities bears out this conclusion. The griffin and the lion remained in the service of Apollo.

FIG. 29.—HATHORIC URAEUS PILLAR AND CYPRO-MYCENAEAN AND ORIENTAL ANALOGIES.
1. Egyptian Uraeus Pillar. 2 and 3. Cypro-Mycenaean Comparisons. 4. Dual Uraeus Staff of Istar.

It is further noteworthy that a certain mystic duality visible in the Hathoric pillars was taken over in a simpler form by Cypriote religion. The head-piece of Hathor represents the meaning of her name as the 'House of Horus,' and may therefore be considered as at the same time implying the internal presence of her divine son. It is sufficient to compare the annexed figure (Fig. 29, 1) of a Hathoric pillar with an uraeus snake curving up and confronting it on either side, taken from an Egyptian signet[1] of seventeenth or eighteenth Dynasty date with the two following designs of the Cypro-Mycenaean class,[2] the latter, to make complete the comparison, on a flat rectangular bead-seal of the same form as the Egyptian. In both of these derivative designs we see a double column. In Fig. 29, 2, the incurving Hathoric sprays become two snakes whose coils on another Cypro-Mycenaean

---

[1] Found in an intrusive burial at Kahun, Petrie, *Kahun, Gurob, and Hawara*, Pl. X. 79, and p. 32.

[2] Fig. 29, 2 is from a cylinder, Cesnola, *Salaminia*, Pl. XII. 7. Fig. 29, 3 *op. cit.* p. 145, Fig. 128. Both are from Salamis.

cylinder are prolonged down the lower member of the column. In Fig. 29, 3 the pillar becomes quite symmetrical in its duality with an intervening slab to divide its two portions. Both of these Cypro-Mycenaean pillars are surmounted by a halo of rays, the original suggestion of which has been already noted. The radiation in itself connects them with divinities of light, a guardian griffin indeed sits before the pillar on the cylinder from which Fig. 29, 2 is taken. In some cases the double pillar is surmounted by a double halo of rays[1] emphasising the dual aspect of the divinity.

The Egyptian religious element in some of these Cypriote double columns is clear. But there is sufficient evidence to show that there was also an oriental class of dual pillars which may have influenced the cult forms of the island at an even earlier period. There occurs, for instance, a type consisting of double cones in reversed positions, their apexes separated by a cross-piece,[2] which is also found on Babylonian cylinders. Another oriental type of divided pillar must be regarded as in part at least of Egyptian origin. This is the staff or small pillar with a globular break in the middle of the stem and two uraeus snakes curving up on either side which so frequently occurs in the hands of Istar on late Babylonian cylinders[3] (Fig. 29, 4). The uraei are here a certain indication of borrowing from the Egyptian side. Their symmetrical grouping recalls the snakes of the Hathoric staff or pillar already cited and forms a recurring feature in the derivative Cypriote types. The pillar stem of the Assyrian sacred tree frequently shows the same central division. But the Assyrian tree itself is in its origin a palmette column belonging to the same family as the eighteenth Dynasty Egyptian, and the earlier Cypro-Mycenaean class.

The pillar image of divinity as will be shown in connexion with the column in the Lions' Gate scheme has this distinct advantage over the anthropomorphic type that the same pillar can represent a divinity either in a male or female aspect or can become the material resting place of either member of a divine pair. Still more obvious facilities were offered by divided columns like the above for the needs of a dual cult. It gave easy expression to the Semitic religious conception of bi-sexual godhead. So too in Cyprus it might well convey the idea expressed by the alternative impersonation of Aphroditê and Aphroditos. The aniconic religion at least obviated such grotesque creations of the later cult as the 'bearded Aphroditê.'

---

[1] A Cypro-Mycenaean cylinder in the Ashmolean Museum.

[2] Dr. Ohnefalsch-Richter, *Kypros*, &c. p. 182, has perhaps rightly recognised this type in the pairs of double axe-like figures grouped on either side of a serpent on a Cypriote cylinder (Cesnola, *Salaminia*, p. 128. Fig. 118). He uses the word 'Chammanim' in connection with these double cones.

[3] C. Menant, *Glyptique Orientale*, i. p. iii. Fig. 99, p. 165, Fig. 102; *Cat. De Clercq.* Pl. XVI. Fig. 160. This class of haematite

cylinders is common in Syria and Cilicia, and a good example from Cyprus exists in the British Museum. The double staff with the *uraei* also occurs in a separate form between two figures of Hea-Bani contending with a bull, bearing the names of the Sun God Samas and apparently his consort (Menant, *Cat. De Clercq.* i. Pl. VIII. Fig. 68 and p. 57), where, however, the comparison with the symbol of Istar is missed, and the object described as a 'candelabrum.'

To the bi-sexual Hermaphroditos indeed the pillar form clung down to much later times.

§ 19.—*The Egyptian Element in the Animal Supporters of Mycenaean Trees and Columns.*

Nothing is itself more contrary to the native genius of Mycenaean art, so free and naturalistic in its home-born impulses, than the constrained and schematic pose of the animals and mythical monsters that in this group of designs appear as guardians or supporters of the sacred trees and columns. But it is precisely because these attendant animals are here conceived of as performing a religious function that they take this heraldic and traditional form. It is usual to regard the pairs of opposed animals as due to oriental influence. It can be shown, indeed, that the reduplicated forms of mythical monsters are in some cases the natural result of the process of cylinder engraving as practised in Chaldaea at a very remote period. Certain types of the same class that appear on Mycenaean gems, such as the bulls with crossed bodies, the hero holding two lions in reverse positions, or the lions by themselves similarly grouped must unquestionably be due to Babylonian prototypes. But it must not be forgotten that in Egypt, too, these opposed heraldic pairs are a very ancient tradition. In the fresco of the prae-dynastic tomb, recently discovered by Mr. Green at Hierakonpolis, a hero is seen struggling with two symmetrically opposed bulls in a manner which, except for its rudeness, exactly recalls figures of Gilgames and Ecbani on Chaldaean cylinders. Paired heraldic animals are found in some hieroglyphic types, and on a monument of the sixth Dynasty two goats are seen symmetrically grouped on either side of a tree.[1] On a fragmentary vase of the black ware characteristic of the twelfth and thirteenth Dynasties, two pairs of goats are seen acting as heraldic supporters, in the one case of a palm-tree, in the other of a vine. It appears, moreover, that Egyptian models of parallel schemes found their way on scarabs, at least as far as Rhodes, and could be copied by the Mycenaean engraver on his native shores. In the well of Kameiros, together with a scarab bearing apparently the cartouche of Thothmes III,[2] was found another example [3]—in steatite of rude work—on which two bovine animals each with the Ankh symbol beneath it stand symmetrically facing a palm-tree. In considering the Lions' Gate scheme we shall have occasion to note the parallel grouping of Ra and Ma before the solar obelisk and of the two lions supporting the sun's disk on the horizon.[4] We have, moreover, direct evidence that, in another shape, the Mycenaeans were familiarised with the Egyptian scheme of a sacred pillar between heraldically opposed animals. This scheme is, in fact, very frequent about the time of the eighteenth Dynasty under the form of

---

[1] Lepsius, *Denkmäler*, iv. Taf. 108, 111; cited by Riegl, *Stilfragen*, p. 40.

[2] *B.M. Gem Cat.* No. 144.

[3] *Ib.* No. 142. The animals are there described as wolves; to me they seem clearly oxen, though roughly drawn; *Myk. Vasen* Pl. E, 39.

[4] See below Fig. 42.

the Tat pillar between two symmetrically grouped uraeus snakes, and a scarab[1] with this design was found in one of the group of Mycenaean graves at Ialysos, from another of which a lentoid gem representing the column between two lions was brought to light. At Tel-el-Amarna, where Egyptian and Mycenaean culture find more than one point of contact, scarabs with similar designs of the Tat and Uraei also occurred.

It is further to be noted that the distribution of the guardian animals as regards the trees and foliate pillars on the one hand and the architectural columns and bases on the other seems to follow a division already perceptible among their Egyptian prototypes. Setting aside the mythical monsters which to a certain extent at all events seem common to both groups we find the heraldic grouping of oxen and goats confined to the trees or tree pillars. The lions alone are associated with the structural columns and altar bases just as in Egyptian religious art we find them exclusively acting as supporters of the symbol of the sun on the horizon.

The general conclusion to which we are led is that the animals symmetrically posed and paired before trees and pillars in these Mycenaean schemes represent a tradition borrowed from Egyptian sources. The conventional scheme had certain religious associations and was therefore adopted for animals performing sacral functions as guardians of holy trees and baetylic columns. It has been already noted that several of the monstrous forms represented in the Mycenaean series like the Sphinx, the Kriosphinx, and the Griffin are themselves Egyptian creations and of their nature divine. In other cases the sacred character of the animal is indicated by the conventional pose of ancient tradition.

§ 20.—*Sacred Trees and Foliated Pillars with Heraldically Posed Animals.*

The sacred tree, when it occurs on Mycenaean designs of the heraldic class at present under consideration, is generally more or less conventionalised in form and often shades off into the foliated pillar. A somewhat naturalistic example (Fig. 30) may be cited from a lentoid gem found in a tomb of the Lower Town of Mycenae in 1895.[2] The tree here rises from a kind of base and on either side with their heads turned towards it are two wild goats or agrimia back to back, who in each case rest their fore feet on a structure rising in two high steps.

In Fig. 31 from a lentoid gem found at Palaeokastro on the easternmost point of Crete[3] we see a single wild goat in a similar heraldic attitude before a tree of conventional type with side sprays and trefoil crest. Behind the agrimi is a smaller animal with the feet and hindquarters of an ape which seems to be in the act of springing on it. It suggests the Cynocephalus that appears in the field of some Babylonian cylinders. To the

---

[1] *Myk. Vasen*, Taf. E, 2.
[2] A banded agate.

[3] A striated chalcedony. I obtained it on the site in 1898.

right of this is an object like an impaled triangle which has probably some religious significance and occurs elsewhere in sacral subjects.[1] The two-horned object placed at the foot of the tree pillar will be seen to be the

FIG. 30.—SACRED TREE AND WILD GOATS ON LENTOID GEM FROM MYCENAE (⅔).

characteristic concomitant of Mycenaean cult referred to above as 'the horns of consecration.' Its appearance in this place is of considerable importance as affording a proof that we have here to deal with a conventional represen-

FIG. 31.—SACRED PALM AND WILD GOAT, LENTOID, PALAEOKASTRO, CRETE (⅔).

FIG. 32.—TREE PILLAR AND ANIMALS LIKE RED DEER : LENTOID GEM, GOULÀS, CRETE (⅔).

tative of a sacred tree. It indicates the holy character of the tree before which it is placed as in other cases its occurrence at the foot of the pillars in Mycenaean shrines declare them to be the aniconic images of divinity.

---

[1] See below, p. 61.

Had this design been fully carried out it would have doubtless included a second wild goat as a supporter on the other side of the tree. From its schematic attitude this belongs to the same class as the opposed pairs of sacral animals.

Fig. 32 [1] presents an example of a tree or tree-pillar with conventional, palm-like foliage, and a fluted columnar shaft supported by what to judge from their horns are a pair of red deer. Both this and the two preceding designs show curious points of resemblance to the stele found by Count Malvasia at Bologna in a cemetery of the Villanova class.[2] Upon this stele a conventional palm-column in two stages is seen between two calf-like supporters whose heads, as in the case of Fig. 34 below, are turned away from the column.

A good illustration of the fleur-de-lys type of foliated pillar akin to those of Mycenaean Cyprus and contemporary Egypt is supplied by a gold signet ring from the Lower Town of Mycenae (Fig. 33).[3] Here we see a fluted

FIG. 33.—FLEUR-DE-LYS PILLAR · AND CONFRONTED SPHINXES, ON GOLD SIGNET RING, MYCENAE (¾)

pillar resting upon a bowl-like base, the foliage of which still suggests the original iris type. On either side of this 'hyacinthine' column and con- fronting it is seated a female Sphinx of the Mycenaean type, with double crest and curling locks visible on the bosom. The sleeved appearance of the upper part of their forelegs is a frequent characteristic of oriental Sphinxes,

---

[1] It was found at Goulàs in Crete (cf. *Goulàs, the City of Zeus*, p. 24. The stone is a lentoid, of transparent and milky chalce- dony.

[2] Gozzadini, *Di alcuni Sepolcri della Necro- poli Felsinea*, p. 20; Undset, *Zeitschrift für Ethnologie*, B. xv. p. 214. S. Reinach, *An- thropologie*, 1893, p. 707, and *Les Celtes dans les Vallées du Pô et du Danube*, pp. 165, 166, gives a conjectural restoration (Fig. 93) of the monument as inserted in the tympanum

of a gate of prehistoric Felsina. A comparison of the stone with other sepulchral stelae in the Museum at Bologna has, however, convinced me that it belongs to the same class. Several of these terminate above in conventional palmettes like so many of the later Greek stelae.

[3] Cf. Perrot et Chipiez, *L'Art*, &c. vi. Fig. 428, 22; Furtwängler, *Ant. Gemmen*, iii. p. 42, Fig. 17.

and is undoubtedly a feature taken over from the hawk of the Egyptian Sun-God Horus. The Sphinx itself belongs, of course, to the same solar cycle, though in Egypt it is rarely of the female sex. Elsewhere we shall see the Sphinx, like the Griffin, as a guardian of the architectural column.

A very similar type of foliated pillar with two young bulls or oxen symmetrically attached on either side, occurs on another gold signet ring from Mycenae.[1] A close parallel, again, to this is presented by a beautifully engraved ring cut out of a single piece of rock crystal which was found some years since at Mycenae (Fig. 34).[2] Two couchant bulls with their heads turned back are tethered to the foliate pillar in the same way as in the preceding example, the only difference being that two additional sprays of the same conventional kind rise from behind their backs. On a lentoid

FIG. 34.—PILLAR TREE WITH YOUNG BULLS ATTACHED : CRYSTAL SIGNET RING, MYCENAE (²⁄₁)

bead seal[3] two animals, one a bull and the other a wild goat, are symmetrically ranged beside a pair of conventional tree-pillars with spiral shafts and tri-foliate sprays.

§ 21.—*Architectural Columns with Animal Supporters: the Lions' Gate Type.*

The most conspicuous example of purely architectural columns with animal supporters is the tympanum relief of the Lions' Gate at Mycenae (Fig. 35) But in this case the position of the column, as if fulfilling an architectural, and at the same time a decorative purpose, has to a great extent diverted archaelogical students from its true religious significance.[4] The lions

---

[1] From Tomb 25 of the Lower Town. Tsuntas, 'Εφ. 'Αρχ. 1889, Pl. X. 43, and pp. 143 and 179. Tsuntas describes the animals as horses, δύο ἵπποι (ἄγριοι); but short horns are clearly discernible.

[2] In my own collection; hitherto unpublished.

[3] Of agate, from Tomb 10 of the Lower Town Mycenae. Tsuntas, 'Εφ. 'Αρχ. 1888, Pl. X. 7 and p. 140; Furtwängler, *Ant. Gemmen*, iii. 27.

[4] M. Salomon Reinach, however, has shown himself alive to its true significance, and in his ' Mirage Orientale (*Anthropologie*, iv.

have not been recognised as the sacred animals and companions of a tutelary divinity, but merely as symbolic figures of the military might of those who held the walls of the citadel, and as a challenge to their foes.[1] The column itself and the architrave and beam-ends that it supports have been taken, with the altars below, to stand for the Palace of the Mycenaean Kings.[2] Some of the earlier writers, indeed, advanced views on the subject of this relief, which in certain respects very nearly approximated to the true explanation. Colonel Mure,[3] and after him Gerhard,[4] and Curtius,[5] saw in the column

FIG. 35.—TYMPANUM RELIEF OF LIONS' GATE, MYCENAE.

between the Lions a 'symbol' of Apollo Agyieus, and Göttling regarded it as a Herm.[6] But such comparisons have been wholly set aside by most later critics.

1893, p. 705 and p. 730) not only rightly describes the column as an aniconic image, but uses the fact of the appearance of the Goddess in its place on the monument of Arslan Kaya as an argument for the later date of the Phrygian relief.

[1] Perrot et Chipiez, *Grèce Primitive*, p. 800.

[2] Brunn, *Griechische Kunstgeschichte* (1893) pp. 26-28 ; Perrot et Chipiez, *op. cit.* p. 801.

[3] *Ueber die königlichen Grabmäler des heroischen Zeitalters*, *Rhein. Museum*, vi. (1838), p. 256. Col. Mure thought the lions

were wolves, and brought Apollo Lykeios into connexion with them.

[4] *Mykenische Alterthümer* (10ter Programm, Berliner Winckelmannsfest, Berlin, 1850) p. 10.

[5] *Peloponnesos* (Gotha, 1852), ii. 405, and *Gr. Geschichte*, i. 116.

[6] *N. Rhein. Museum*, i. (1842) p. 161. Göttling notes the correspondence between the Mycenaean column growing smaller towards its base and the Hermae pillars—a pregnant observation.

The fact that the column had a capital, and in this case actually supported a roof, was pronounced by Dr. Adler to be fatal to the view that any aniconic form of a divinity could be here represented, 'all such idols having a free ending as a cone, a meta or a phallus.'[1] It has been shown above, however, that the idea of the divine column as a 'Pillar of the House,' and actually performing a structural function is deeply rooted in this early religion, and finds parallels both on the Semitic and the Egyptian side. In the succeeding sections a series of Mycenaean shrines will be described in which the stone pillar which is the aniconic form of the divinity is represented as actually contributing to prop up the capstone or lintel. In the Lions' Gate and kindred types where the column stands for the support of a building, the capital and impost are in fact required to bring out the full idea of the upholding spiritual power. The divinity here is the 'pillar of Mycenae,' even as Hector is described by Pindar,[2] as the 'pillar of Troy.'

The Lions' Gate scheme is found, sometimes in an abbreviated form, on a series of Mycenaean engraved stones and rings, some examples of which are given below, associated with the same sacred animals. In other cases we find the pillar, or simply the altar base, guarded by Sphinxes, Griffins, or Kriosphinxes.

On the ivory plaque from the Tholos tomb, at Menidi, two Sphinxes stand[3] on either side of a Mycenaean column. A small figure of ivory from Mycenae[4] represents a Sphinx resting both forelegs on the capital of a short column. In Fig. 33 we have already seen Sphinxes as guardians of a tree pillar.

A lentoid gem from Mycenae (Fig. 36)[5] gives the best architectural parallel to the Lions' Gate pillar, save that here we see a pair of Griffin supporters in place of the lions. The column here rests on a single altar base instead of two.

FIG. 36.—PILLAR WITH GRIFFIN SUPPORTERS; LENTOID, MYCENAE (¾).

It is spirally fluted, and above the capital is seen a part of the entablature with the round ends of the transverse beams as on the tympanum reliefs.

---

[1] *Arch. Zeitung*, 1865, p. 6, 'Alle solche Idole niemals in der Form einer mit einem Capitell geschmückten Säule (welche hier sogar eine Decke trägt) sondern stets frei beendigt als Conus, Meta, Phallus erscheinen.'

[2] *Ol.* ii. 145, Τροίας ἄμαχον ἀστραβῆ κίονα.

[3] Lolling, *Kuppelgrab von Menidi*, p. 20. Perrot et Chipiez, *L'Art*, &c., p. 528, Fig. 208.

[4] Tsuntas, 'Εφ. 'Αρχ. 1887, Pl. XIII. Ἐ, and p. 171. P. et C. vi. p. 833, Fig. 417, where however it is erroneously described as 'from the Acropolis of Athens.'

[5] Tsuntas, Μυκῆναι, Pl. V. 6; Ts. and Manatt, *Myc. Age*, p. 254, Fig. 131. Furtw. *Ant. Gemm.* vol. iii. p. 44, Fig. 18.

The Griffins, with their heads turned back, are attached to the upper part of the column like watch dogs by a thong or chain, a constantly recurring feature in these designs.

A scheme closely allied to the above, in which, however, the altar-base appears without the column, is supplied by a jasper lentoid from Tomb 42

FIG. 37.—DOUBLE-BODIED KRIOSPHINX WITH FORE-FEET ON BASE: LENTOID GEM, MYCENAE (¾)

FIG. 38.—DOUBLE-BODIED LION WITH FORE-FEET ON BASE: LENTOID GEM, MYCENAE (¾).

of the Lower Town, Mycenae (Fig. 37).[1] Here we see a composite animal, in which the bodies of two opposed lions meet in the single head of a ram, resting its forefeet on the base. To the right is a symbol like a pole transfixing a triangle, which has been already referred to as a frequent concomitant of Mycenaean religious scenes, and may perhaps represent

FIG. 39.—LIONS' GATE TYPE ON GOLD SIGNET RING, MYCENAE (¾).

some kind of 'Ashera,' making up in this case for the absence of the architectural pillar. The composite monster itself of which this is the

[1] Tsuntas, 'Εφ. 'Αρχ. 1888, Pl. X. 30, and p. 178; P. et C. Fig. 428, 17; Furtw. Ant. Gemm. Pl. III. 24. He describes the monsters (vol. ii. p. 23) as 'zwei geflügelte und gehörnte Löwen.'

reduplicated form, is, in fact, the Egyptian Kriosphinx, here, however, fitted with wings according to the Mycenaean practice. At Karnak huge Kriosphinxes—with the head of a ram and the body of a lion—guard the avenue of the Theban lunar God Khonsu. An analogous design, representing a double-bodied lion, with a single head, his forelegs resting on a similar base, occurs on another lentoid from Mycenae (Fig. 38.)[1]

On rings and gems, indeed, the more usual guardians of the sacred pillar are lions. A gold signet-ring from Mycenae (Fig. 39)[2] shows a pillar with a somewhat broad entablature to which two lions are attached by chains round their necks. The animals look back at the column, and two objects of uncertain character attached to the end of the entablature on either side, hang down in front of their noses. These objects, which in their general outline somewhat resemble the two alabaster knots found in the fourth Acropolis grave at Mycenae,[3] have perhaps a sacral character, for, on the

FIG. 40.—LIONS' GATE TYPE ON LENTOID GEM, ZERO, CRETE ($\frac{2}{1}$).

Heraeum gem,[4] two similar are seen on either side of a bull's head, above which is the symbolic double axe.

A cornelian lentoid from grave 33 of the Cemetery of Ialysos[5] shows a rude and straggling design of a column with two lion supporters looking outwards. Another hitherto unpublished variant of the type is supplied by a brown cornelian lentoid gem (Fig. 40) obtained by me at Zêro in Eastern Crete. Two lions are here symmetrically seated back to

[1] From tomb 8 of the lower town of Mycenae, Tsuntas, 'Εφ. 'Αρχ. 1888, Pl. X. 2, and p. 175 ; P. et C. vi. Pl. XVI. 20 ; Furtw. *Ant. Gemm.* Pl. III. 23.

[2] Formerly in the Tyszkiewicz Collection, at present in my own. Fröhner, *Coll. Tyszk.*, Pl. I. 3.

[3] Schliemann, *Mycenae*, p. 242, Fig. 352.

[4] See above p. 11.

[5] B. M. *Gem Cat.* Pl. A. 106 ; Curtius, *Wappengebrauch und Wappenstil*, p. 111 ; Furtw. u. Löschke, *Myk. Vas.* Pl. E. 6, pp. 15 and 75 ; Furtw. *Ant. Gemm.* Pl. III. 20.

back with their heads turned towards the column above which are some traces of the round beam ends of the entablature.

The base on which the two lions rest their forelegs on the lentoid gem represented in Fig. 41[1] must not be confounded with the usual altar base seen in Figs. 37 and 38 above, the typical feature of which is the incurving sides. It is essentially columnar, and its true meaning has been shown in an earlier section of this work.[2] It represents, in fact, one of the baetylic tables of offering, which seem to be a special characteristic of this early cult in Crete where the intaglio itself was found. The component elements of this sacral type are the central baetylic column and an altar slab placed upon it with four smaller legs to support it at the corners. In the field above is seen a rayed sun.

Like the tree pillar with its heraldic supporters, the Lions' Gate scheme

Fig. 41.—Confronted Lions with Fore-feet on Baetylic Base, Lentoid, Crete ($\frac{3}{1}$).

with its central architectural column or altar base shows very distinct analogies to some of the Cypriote types, the central feature of which is the rayed symbolic column. The parallelism becomes still closer when we find, in both cases, lions, Griffins and Sphinxes among the most frequent guardians or supporters of the divine pillar, though in Mycenaean Cyprus they are also depicted as actually adoring the aniconic image. It has been shown above that in the case of the Cypriote cylinders the attendant

---

[1] Furtwängler u. Löschke, *Myk. Vasen*, Pl. E, 11 ; Furtw., *Geschnittene Steine* (Berlin Cat.) Pl. I. 34; P. et C. vi. Pl. XVI. 11 ; Furtw., *Ant. Gemm.*, Pl. III. 22. The stone is a dark red steatite.

[2] See above p. 18 *seqq.*

F

monsters and, to a certain extent, the symbolic column itself, are taken from an Egyptian solar cycle, and the inference has been drawn that the aniconic pillars among the Mycenaeans of Cyprus were identified with divinities having some points in common with the Sun-Gods Ra, or Horus, and Hathor, the Great Mother.

The rayed sun which in Fig. 41 appears in the field above the confronted lions, certainly corroborates the view that in the Aegean countries the aniconic pillars, which appear in a similar conjunction, were also connected with solar divinities. The pillar here indeed is, as already noted, of a purely indigenous shape, and cannot itself, like the symbolic Cyprian types with their reminiscences of palmette capitals and Hathoric scrolls, be directly traced to an Egyptian prototype. The Nilotic connexion has nevertheless left its traces in these Mycenaean types. We recall the frequent appearance in Egyptian religious art of opposed figures in special association with the solar symbols and pillars of the sun. Thus we see the squatting, confronted figures of Ra with his hawk's head and Ma with her feather crest on either side of the Sun-God's obelisk, and in

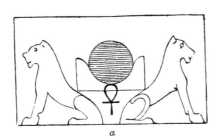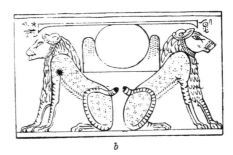

          a   *b*

FIG. 42*a*, *b*.—LION SUPPORTERS OF EGYPTIAN SOLAR DISK.

other cases the figure of the sun's disk on the horizon is supported by two lions seated back to back (Fig. 42 *a* and *b*). To a certain extent the Lions' Gate scheme may itself be regarded as a combination of these two types. The column on the altar is a free indigenous translation of the obelisk rising on its base which really represents the 'Mastaba' or sepulchral chapel. The back to back position of the two lions is literally reproduced in Figs. 39 and 40, and where, as in Figs. 37 and 41, the bodies of the lions are turned towards the central pillar, their heads are averted as if in deference to the same religious tradition. The monsters here are not so much simply adorants as on the Cyprian cylinders, and therefore regarding the sacred pillar, but are guardians looking out and away from it for possible enemies. On the Lions' Gate itself they naturally look forward along the avenue of approach.

It must, in fact, be clearly recognised that the scheme of the pillar and guardian monsters as it appears in Mycenaean art on the Lions' Gate and in other kindred designs is, like the Griffins and Sphinxes that often form part of it, essentially of Egyptian derivation. It is translated into indigenous terms and applies, doubtless, to indigenous divinities, but it is reasonable to suspect in the latter some points of resemblance to the divinities of light with which the parallel religious types seem to have been specially associated in the Nile valley.

§ 22.—*Anthropomorphic Figures of Divinities substituted for the Baetylic Column in the Lions' Gate Scheme.*

Attention has been called above to the Mycenaean practice, in depicting religious scenes, of supplementing the design of the sacred tree or pillar that formed the material object of the cult by placing beside it a figure of the divinity itself as visible to the mind's eye of the worshippers. The

Fig. 43 —Male Divinity between Lions on Lentoid Gem, Kydonia, Crete (?).

God or Goddess is seen in actual converse beneath the holy tree, seated beside or even on the shrine, or even at times in the act of descending beside the altar block, or in front of the pillar image. It has been remarked above that this pictorial expedient of religious art must be regarded as symptomatic of a process of transition in the rendering of the aniconic idol itself, which in the succeeding historic period was gradually moulded into anthropomorphic form.

But besides this supplementary representation of the divinity side by side with its tree or pillar shape there is evidence of another method of satisfying the realistic cravings of a more advanced religious stage. This is the actual substitution of the God or Goddess in human guise in the place of the aniconic image. It is possible, for instance in the case of the Lions' Gate scheme, to give a series of examples in which a divinity is introduced

F 2

between the lion supporters in place of the column. We have here in fact, pictorially anticipated, a religious grouping which later, as will be seen from certain types of Apollo, Kybelê and the Asiatic Artemis, attached itself to the cult images.

These religious schemes in which the divinity simply replaces the pillar must be distinguished from some other designs, also exemplified by Mycenaean signets, bearing a certain superficial resemblance to them, in which a male hero is seen in the act of grappling with a pair of lions. These have another origin and should more probably be regarded as adaptations of the familiar Chaldaean type of Gilgames. Sometimes as in the design on a gold signet ring we see two heroes engaged in the same struggle,[1] a scene also taken from the Babylonian repertory.

But a very different impression is given by the type on an unpublished Mycenaean gem (Fig. 43),[2] discovered in the immediate neighbourhood of

Fig. 44.—Female Divinity between Lions on Amygdaloid Gem, Mycenae (⅔).

Canea, on or near the site of the ancient Kydonia. Here we see a male figure, his arms symmetrically extended, with two lions heraldically opposed on either side. The stiff upright figure here with the legs together is an almost perfect substitute for the central column, and the horizontally extended arms directly suggest the entablature of the Lions' Gate scheme. It is in fact the literal translation of the pillar image into human shape.

A variant of this design in which the standing figure grasps the two lion supporters by the necks is seen on a serpentine lentoid, unfortunately much damaged by fire, which was found in one of the Greek islands.[3] In this case

---

[1] In the Museum at Péronne.

[2] A white agate lentoid ; in my collection. Found in 1894.

[3] In the Berlin Museum. Furtw., *Geschn Steine*, No. 9.

the forelegs of the lions rest on two bases, a feature which brings the scheme into the closest relation with that of the Lions' Gate.

The central figure also appears in female form. On a fine agate gem recently found at Mycenae (Fig. 44)[1] a Goddess is seen in the usual costume holding up her two hands in an evenly balanced attitude between a lion and a lioness. Another intaglio (Fig. 45),[2] on a lentoid of pale yellow cornelian which forms the bezel of a gold ring, shows the Goddess seated on a lion's head, while on either side of her two lions are heraldically posed looking backwards. It will be seen that the attitude of the lions is directly borrowed from the aniconic scheme in which they rest their feet on an altar or small pillar, while the Goddess herself is represented armless and in an unusual sack-like costume as if something of her columnar form still affected the artist's imagination.

It will be noticed that these figures of the Goddess between her lion

Fig. 45.—Seated Goddess between Lions on Lentoid Ring-Stone (¾).

supporters supply almost exact parallels, though of a considerably earlier date, and in a purely Mycenaean style, to a well-known Phrygian monument which has hitherto afforded the best illustration of the religious conception underlying the original tympanum relief.

In Phrygia, where the tradition of the Mycenaean scheme seems to have been long maintained in the tympanum groups above the rock-hewn tombs,

[1] In my collection.
[2] From the collection of the late Sir Wollaston Franks, to whose kindness was due the cast from which Fig. 45 was drawn. The ring is now with the rest of his collection in the British Museum. It was originally in the hands of a Swiss collector, but the provenience is unknown. From the style of cutting it is probably of Cretan fabric, and in support of this view it may be mentioned that pale yellow cornelians of the same class are common in a rough state in Eastern Crete.

the frequent design of the lions on either side of a column [1] is replaced inside a sepulchral chamber described by Professor Ramsay at Arslan Kaia by two lions or lionesses in the usual heraldic attitude on either side of a rude image of Kybelê.[2] It is, in fact, little more than the earlier columnar form of the Goddess slightly hewn,[3] and we here see the cult image coming as it were to life and first putting on a human shape.

A distinction must indeed be observed between the two cases. The Phrygian image belongs to a much later date and represents the partial anthropomorphization of the actual cult pillar, a stage of which in still later, Greco-Roman days the Syrian and Anatolian shrines supply so many examples. The figures on the Mycenaean gems, on the other hand, must be rather regarded as the purely pictorial impersonation of the Goddess as seen by the eye of faith. It may be, as suggested above, that the columnar cult shape had, to a certain extent, influenced the pictorial representation in the last mentioned design with the seated Goddess. On the whole, however, the figure is distinctly human, the feet are given as well as the head, the curves of the seated body and the flounced raiment below. There is nothing here resembling the very imperfect anthropomorphization of the pillar idol that we find in the relief of Arslan Kaia. The one is an anthropomorphic figure of the Goddess slightly affected by the columnar cult image, the other is a pillar image slightly modified by the anthropomorphic ideal form. With the Mycenaeans, as clearly pointed out, all the evidence goes to show that the cult-image itself was still a simple pillar or sacred stone.

The divine figure on these Mycenaean gems is truly a Lion Goddess, closely analogous, at any rate, to the Mother Kybelê—*Matar Kubile*—of the Phrygian monument. The attitude of the lions indeed in the last example placing their forepaws upon the seated figure of the Goddess corresponds with that which at a much later date than the Arslan Kaia monument continued to be associated with Kybelê and Rhea.

On the cylinder seals of the Cypro-Mycenaean class there is also evidence of a Lion Goddess. On an example from Salamis a seated female divinity holds in her left hand a bird, perhaps a dove, and places her right on a low pillar, representing her baetylic form, behind which is a rampant lion who, resting one paw on the pillar-idol, raises the other in the act of adoration. Lions in the schematic pose of adorants or guardians appear before several of the sacred pillars on these Cyprian cylinders which in some cases at least may

---

[1] See W. M. Ramsay, *Journ. Hellen. Stud.* vol. iii. p. 18 *seqq.* and Plates XVIII., XIX. One group is thus described *loc. cit.* p. 19. 'Over the door is carved an obelisk. On each side of the obelisk a large lion is carved in low relief rampant with its fore-paw on the top of the door.' In this case there was a little cub below each of the lions.

[2] *Journ. Hellen. Stud.* vol. v. (1884), pp. 244, 245.

[3] The true import of this figure was first pointed out by M. Salomon Reinach, 'Mirage Orientale' (*Anthropologie*, iv. 1893, p. 705). M. Reinach justly observes 'cette déesse tient la place de la colonne de Mycènes qui appartient au stage *aniconique* de la civilisation grecque : le monument où l'anthropomorphisme se fait jour est certainement le plus récent des deux.'

be taken to represent the same Goddess. In the case of these Cypriote types we are led from the associated symbols to seek a celestial divinity who, if on the Hellenic side of her being she approaches Dionê, has certain attributes in common with the Egyptian Hathor. It is possible that both in Asia Minor and in prehistoric Greece equally with Mycenaean Cyprus the lion cult may have passed to the 'Great Mother' of the indigenous religions, owing to the near relation in which Hathor the 'Great Mother' of Egyptian cult stood to the Sun-God who was there the special Lord of Lions. In considering the religious subjects on the Cypro-Mycenaean cylinders we shall see to what a large extent the cult of Hathor left its impress on that of the Mycenaean colonists, and the same influence is clearly traceable on the contemporary 'Hittite' art of Anatolia. It would even appear that the turret or mural crown common to the Asiatic Goddess in her several forms is the direct derivative of the 'House of Hor' on the head of Hathor. Kybelê too was a 'Virgo Caelestis,' with sun or moon for her attributes— Mother according to one tradition of Hêlios and Selênê,[1] just as the closely allied Hellenic Rhea is made the Mother of the Cretan Light-God known to the Greeks as Zeus. Her title of Basileia as 'Queen of Heaven' recalls the title of Fanassa applied in Cyprus to Dionê or Aphroditê Urania. Finally the Phrygian Kybelê is the special protectress of cities. The Mycenaean column supports the roof-beams; in her mural crown the Mother Goddess supports the city itself. So far at least as Mycenae itself was concerned, no more appropriate tutelary image could have been found for its citadel gate. As the special patroness of the Tantalidae Kybelê would have been the natural protectress of the city of Pelops, Atreus and Agamemnon.[2]

But, as we have seen, the pillar image between the lions also takes a male form. Moreover, the lion guardians of Egyptian religious art, which, as has already been shown, in reality supplied the starting-point for this very scheme, are bound up with the cult of the male solar divinities Ra and Horus.

The alternative substitution of a male and female divinity for the pillar image of the Lions' Gate scheme recalls a feature in this early aniconic cult to which attention has already been drawn. It is highly probable that the same pillar could in fact become by turns the material dwelling-place of either member of a divine pair. At Paphos, for instance, it could represent either Aphroditê or Aphroditos. The Semitic religious notions,—which may well have had a much wider extension—according to which what is practically the same divine being can present either a male or a female aspect, fitted in admirably with this ancient pillar cult. But in the case of the Lions' Gate itself and of one of the engraved seal-stones cited above, there is a feature which strongly confirms the idea that the column in this case served as the

---

[1] Diodôros, l. iii. c. 57.

[2] Pausanias (iii. 22, 4) mentions a temple and image of Mother Goddess at Akriae in Lakonia, said to be the most ancient shrine of the kind in the Peloponnese, though he adds that the Magnesians, to the north of Sipylos, claim that on Κοδδίνου πέτρα to be the oldest of all and the work of Broteas the son of Tantalos. The special connexion of the cult with the Tantalidae makes its appearance at Mycenae the more probable.

common baetylic materialisation of a pair of divinities. The column of the tympanum is supported by two altar bases, suggestive of a double dedication. Again, on the engraved stone from one of the Greek islands, described above, each of the lions on either side of the male figure places his feet on a separate base, which may be taken to show that they too were the sacred animals of a divine pair. If the lion belonged to Kybelê and Rhea, it is also the sacred animal of the Sun-God with which, under variant names and in various relations, these two divinities are coupled. It is probable that in Mycenaean religion, as in the later Phrygian, the female aspect of divinity predominated, fitting on as it seems to have done to the primitive matriarchal system. The male divinity is not so much the consort as the son or youthful favourite. The relationship is rather that of Rhea than of Hera to Zeus, of Adonis rather than of Arês to Aphroditê. In this connexion it is a noteworthy fact that the great majority of the votaries and adorants in the Mycenaean cult scenes are female figures, and in some cases the Goddess that they attend or worship is visible in anthropomorphic form. In other scenes of a similar nature, where apparently divinities of both sexes are represented, the God is either in the background as on the great Akropolis ring,[1] or holds a secondary place as when he approaches a seated Goddess.[2]

§ 23. *The Mycenaean Daemons in similar Heraldic Schemes.*

An interesting parallel to the substitution of anthropomorphic figures of divinities for the baetylic column between its animal supporters is

FIG. 46.—DAEMON BETWEEN LIONS, LENTOID, MYCENAE.

supplied by a gem recently discovered by Dr. Tsuntas in a tomb of the Lower Town of Mycenae.[3] In this design (Fig. 46) a Mycenaean daemon of the usual type takes the place of the divinity between two lions whose front legs rest on what appear to be two altar bases with incurving sides. On the well known lentoid stone said (probably erroneously) to have been found at Corneto or Orvieto[4] we see the converse of this design, in which an anthropomorphic figure stands between two ewer holding daemons. On the glass paste reliefs, of which illus-

---

[1] Fig. 4 above, p. 10.
[2] See Fig. 51 below.
[3] Thanks to the kindness of Dr. Tsuntas I am able here to reproduce this interesting and hitherto unpublished type.
[4] *Annali dell' Instituto*, 1885, Pl. GH.;

Cook, 'Animal Worship,' *J.H.S.* xiv. (1894) p. 120; Helbig, *Question Mycénienne*, p. 37 (325) Fig. 24; Furtwängler, *Ant. Gemmen*, iii. p. 37 Fig. 16 and p. 38 note, where the alleged provenience is with reason called in question.

trations are given above,[1] we see this anthropomorphic figure replaced
between the same daemonic attendants, in the one case by a square pillar in
the other by a columnar tripod. We have here an additional example of the
alternation of the divinity and the pillar image.

It is impossible in this place to enter on a detailed discussion as to the
true interpretation of these strange Mycenaean daemons. It must be sufficient here to give strong expression to the belief that the explanation first
suggested by Dr. Winter, is in the main the true one, and that they represent
a Mycenaean adaptation of an Egyptian hippopotamus Goddess.[2] The head of
the river horse has been assimilated to that of the lion, and the whole design
including the dorsal mane and appendage has been crossed with the type of
the hippocampus, already familiar in Crete on seals of the prae-Mycenaean
period. The frequent use of this Nilotic type in these heraldic schemes of the
Lions' Gate class is an additional corroboration of the view already expressed,
that the pillar image with animal supporters finds its true origin in Egyptian
religious art. The female hippopotamus Ririt, the image of a constellation
standing in connexion with the 'Haunch,' our 'Charles' Wain,'[3] is the fitting
companion of the solar lions, griffins, sphinxes, and krio-sphinxes which we
have already recognised among the supporters of the Mycenaean pillar
images.

§ 24.—A Mycenaean 'Bethshemesh.'

Among the scenes of adoration of pillars, rayed or otherwise, on Cypro-
Mycenaean cylinders, referred to in section 18, we not unfrequently find two
such pillars introduced, indicating the dual cult of two associated divinities.
A good example of this dual cult
from Salamis is given in Fig. 47.[4]
Here we see two pillars, the taller
of which is rayed, while the other
has a very well-marked dividing slab
between its upper and lower members. These pillars are associated
with two female votaries holding
respectively a goat and an ibex,
while the orb and crescent signs
and the bovine head in the field
above point to a combination of
solar and lunar divinities. It is

FIG. 47.—DUAL PILLAR WORSHIP ON CYPRO-
MYCENAEAN CYLINDER ($\frac{2}{1}$)

natural to infer that these pillars represent severally a God and a Goddess and
in this case the rays seem clearly to distinguish the solar member of this

---

[1] P. 19. · Figs. 13, 14.

[2] Dr. Winter compares Thueris. As noticed
below, her counterpart or double the stellar
Ririt has perhaps a better claim.

[3] See Maspero, *Dawn of Civilisation* (Engl.
Ed.), p. 94.

[4] Cesnola, *Salaminia*, Pl. XIII. No. 29.
The material is haematite.

divine pair.   An interesting parallel to this dual cult is presented by a gold
signet ring, procured by me some years since from the site of Knossos, which
has already been referred to by anticipation as supplying evidence of excep-
tional value regarding the aniconic cult of the Mycenaean world.

The signet ring from the site of Knossos is of a typical Mycenaean form,
with a long oval bezel, set at right angles to the hoop.   It is slightly
worn, but the details of the design are still clearly displayed (Fig. 48).   To
the extreme left of the field, as it appears in the impression, is seen a rocky
steep with plants or small trees growing on it, which may be taken to show
that the scene is laid in a mountainous locality.   Immediately in front of this
is a female figure in the flounced Mycenaean dress and with traces of long
tresses falling down her back.   She stands on a stone platform which reminds
one of the supporting terraces that form the emplacement of buildings in so

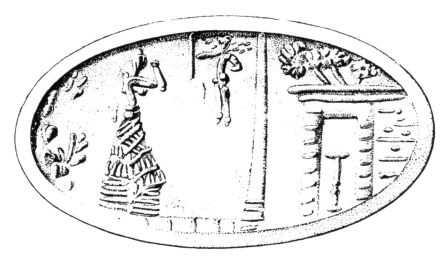

FIG. 48.—DUAL PILLAR WORSHIP ON GOLD SIGNET RING FROM KNOSSOS (⅟).

many of the prehistoric hill cities of Crete.   In this case no doubt we have
to do with an open court, the boundary on one side of which is the terrace
wall, on the other steep rocks—a kind of outer *temenos* of a sanctuary.   This
stone base recurs beneath the cult scenes upon several Mycenaean rings to be
described below.

The female figure who stands here raises her hand in the familiar
attitude of adoration before an obelisk-like pillar, in front of which descends
another small figure, the male sex of which is clearly indicated.   This male
divinity—for so we may venture to call it—holds forth what appears to be
a spear in an attitude which recalls the small figure that hovers above the
group on the gold ring, already referred to, from the Akropolis Treasure of
Mycenae.   In the present case, however, the characteristic shield which
covers the body of the figure is wanting.   The God is entirely nude,
and from his shoulders shoot forth what must certainly be regarded as rays

rather than wings.   To the significance of this feature there will be occasion to return.

Behind the tall obelisk, which shows four rings towards its base, is the gate of a walled enclosure or hypaethral sanctuary, beneath which is seen a second smaller column, consisting of a shaft with a central division, and a capital and base.   Above the cornice of the walls rise the branches of a group of sacred trees, with what appear to be triply divided leaves like those of a fig-tree, and perhaps fruit.   The little dots on the walls of the shrine, arranged in alternating rows, indicate an attempt to represent isodomic masonry.

Apart from the narrower field of comparisons into which this interesting design leads us, its broader anthropological aspects stand clearly revealed. It is a scene of stone or 'baetyl' worship, also partly associated with the cult of trees.   We are here already past that more primitive stage of the religion so well illustrated, for example, among the Melanesians, in which any stone or rock that strikes a man's fancy may become the local habitation of a ghost or spirit.   On the Knossian ring we see stone pillars of an artificial kind, and belonging to a more formalised worship, though still essentially of the same class.   The obelisk, here, is literally, as in the case of the Beth-el set up by Jacob, 'God's house,' and the God is seen actually in the act of being brought down by the ritual incantation of his votary to his earthly tenement of stone.

The obelisk with the God descending before it is only one of a pair of sacred pillars contained in the same cult scene.   It represents the male form of the aniconic image, and to the character of its divine attributes we shall have occasion to return.   The second and lower column, standing apparently in the doorway of the hypaethral shrine, possibly, however, intended to be looked on as set up within its enclosure, may with great probability be regarded as a female form of divinity, or, at any rate, a deity in which the female aspect preponderated.

We are struck, in the first place, by the interesting parallel between the position of the pillar under the gate, and that of the aniconic image of the Paphian Aphrodite on much later monuments.   Considering the many centuries that had elapsed between the date when this Mycenaean ring was engraved, and the earliest representations of the Paphian shrine that have come down to us, some divergence in the outline of the stone might naturally be expected.   The columnar form of the Mycenaean type has been softened perhaps by the contamination of oriental examples, into a conical outline. But Cypriote cylinders of Mycenaean date show that in fact a form of aniconic image was at that time in vogue in the island, absolutely identical with that on our ring.

The distinguishing features of the pillar visible in the doorway on the Knossian ring are the broad base and capital, and a double swelling at the centre, which divides the shaft into two.   In this respect we have before us a close parallel to the double pillars, rayed, or otherwise, on the Cypro-Mycenaean cylinders described in the preceding section.

A further highly interesting point of comparison is supplied by the fact that in the Mycenaean seals of Cyprus, as on the Knossian ring, this divided pillar makes its appearance as one of a pair. In the example already given in Fig. 47, a short pillar with a central division and having above it a bovine head, is associated with another higher column, from the summit of which issue rays. The pillars are here attended by flounced votaries like that of the Cretan signet, and the combined symbol of the orb and crescent sufficiently reveals the character of the cult. The bovine head above the shorter pillar in this case probably indicates a lunar connexion.

It can hardly be doubted, indeed, that in the case of the Cypriote examples the female divinity, thus represented in aniconic form, is to be identified with the Goddess whose cult was in later times specially connected with Paphos. The various associations in which the stone pillar and the votaries associated with it appear on the cylinders clearly betray her true character. The star and crescent,[1] the rays which generally issue from the stone itself, point to her in her character of a luminary of the heavens, Aphroditê Urania. In one case the same figure of a lion in the attitude of adoration that is seen on other cylinders before the rayed pillar [2] stands behind the Goddess herself, who is here seated on a throne in her character of Fanassa, and holds a dove in her hand.[3] The cult of Aphroditê under the name of Ariadnê was also known in Cyprus and it is in this Cretan form that we should most naturally recognise the female consort of the warrior Light-God on the Knossian signet.

On another Cyprian stone—a rectangular bead or 'tabloid' of steatite [4]— we find the same conjunction of the double form of the stone pillar (Fig. 49). On one side is a divided column, in this case rayed above, which evidently corresponds to the female divinity. On the other side is a more obelisk-like column on a double pedestal with rays issuing on every side, which shows distinct points of affinity with the obelisk on the Knossian ring, and here, too, we may infer that it answers to the male member of a divine pair. On a parallel bead-seal the double rayed column of the female divinity is coupled on the reverse side with a rayed orb in place of the obelisk. The solar attribution could not be more clearly indicated.

In the Cypro-Mycenaean versions of the male pillar we see it sur-mounted by a halo of rays. On the Cretan signet ring the same element is supplied by the rays that issue from the shoulders of the descending God. There can be little doubt that this method of expressing the luminous character of the divinity was borrowed from an oriental source. Samas, the Babylonian Sun-God, the Canaanite form of whose name appears as Shemesh, was habitually represented with rays issuing from his shoulders. In the

---

[1] In the cylinder given in *Salaminia*, Pl. XII. No. 8 the star and crescent are seen above the luminous pillar.

[2] *Salaminia*, Pl. XII. Nos. 7 and 8. Some-times the adoring animal is a griffin (*op. cit.*

Pl. XII. No. 5); in one case it has a horse's mane (Pl. XII. No. 6).

[3] *Op. cit.* Pl. XII. No. 14.

[4] *Salaminia*, p. 145, Fig. 138.

obeliskoid pillar of the Cretan ring we have, in fact, a Mycenaean Beth-shemesh, the material place of indwelling for the solar deity that we see here descending upon it, as Beth-el was of the God of Jacob.

The obeliskoid form may itself be regarded as another trace of Egyptian influence on the externals of Mycenaean cult. It is worth remarking that this earlier aspect of the Sun-God as a pyramidal pillar clung in later Greece with great persistence to the cult of Apollo. In the well-known instance of the omphalos at Delphi, the stone, though a lower cone, is probably a variant of the same obelisk-like type. Perhaps, however, the most literal survivals of this form were due to the conservative cult of north-western Greece. On the coins of Ambrakia, of the Illyrian Apollonia and Orikos the obelisk of Apollo appears in a form practically identical with that found on the Cypriote tabloid (Fig. 49) and the Knossian ring. Here, as there, moreover, the elongated upper part of the stone rests on a distinct base, with two or three divisions as in the latter example. May we, perhaps, go a step further in these cases and regard the solar divinity, who is the object of this aniconic cult in Epirus and its borderlands, as a differentiated offshoot of a warrior God, one part of whose being is preserved in the later conception of Zeus? It is certain that at Ambrakia the type is associated with the head of Dionê, the consort of the Pelasgian Zeus.

FIG. 49.—DOUBLE REPRESENTATION OF RAYED PILLARS, ON TABLOID BEAD-SEAL, OLD SALAMIS.

At Amyklae we see the still partly aniconic image of the prae-Dorian Sun-God associated with a similar form of a Goddess known as the armed Aphroditê, who, on her Hellenic side, is indistinguishable from Dionê. On the other hand, the Arcadian Zeus Lykaios is himself the 'God of Light.' In Crete, where this luminous aspect of Zeus is particularly strong, Dionê appears as the 'Mother' of Pasiphaê, the personification of the full moon.

The ancient Light-God of Crete and Arcadia may not improbably turn out to be a deity belonging to the earlier prae-Hellenic population, taken over by later Greek occupants of the country. It is possible that these religious traditions are a survival of a time when, as the Cretan evidence so strongly indicates,[1] a common element had a footing on both the Libyan and Aegean shores. Such a connexion would best explain the deep underlying influence of Egyptian solar cult which our researches so continually encounter. The fact that in one place this Light-God is identified with Apollo, in another with a form of Zeus, of Dionysos, or of Ares, may certainly be regarded as a symptom of adaptation from a foreign source. The true Hellenic Zeus was rather the personification of the luminous sky, and Dionê as she appears in her oldest Epirote home is simply his female form. The fusion of the

---

[1] See 'Further Discoveries of Cretan and Aegean Script; with Proto-Egyptian and Libyan Comparisons,' *J.H.S.* xvii., 1897.

Hellenic Zeus with a divinity representing Mentu Ra, the warrior Sun-God
of Egypt, would naturally favour the assimilation of the female aspect of
both divinities, of Dionê namely and Hathor.

On the ring from Knossos this warrior Sun-God is armed with a spear
or javelin—an archaic trait preserved by the Amyklaean Apollo and the
solar Ares of Thrace. Elsewhere on the great signet ring from Mycenae

FIG. 50.—RAYED SHIELD-BEARING GOD ON PAINTED SARCOPHAGUS, MILATO, CRETE.

and the painted tablet we see a descending armed divinity holding a large
8-shaped body-shield. An interesting piece of Cretan evidence tends to
show that this Mycenaean shield could on occasion be equally associated
with the primitive Light-God of the Knossos signet. In a chambered tomb
at Milato in Crete, the mother-city of the better known Miletos, excavated

by me in 1899, was a painted clay ossuary chest or larnax of the usual Cretan type,—copied, it may be observed, from the wooden chests of contemporary Egypt,— one end of which presented a male figure that must certainly be regarded as a divinity (Fig. 50). With one hand the God holds out a large body-shield of the usual type and from his neck, in this case, immediately above the shoulders issue undulating lines which seem to be the equivalent of the rays of the Knossian divinity and still more nearly of the wavy lines that issue from the shoulders of the Babylonian Samas. It does not appear that he holds anything in the other hand.

§ 25.—*Cult Scenes relating to a Warrior God and his Consort.*

The alternative appearances of the rayed solar God of the Knossian ring or the Milato sarcophagus holding out in the one case a spear, in the other the Mycenaean body-shield, render almost inevitable the comparison of these

Fig. 51.—Armed God and Seated Goddess on Electrum Signet Ring, Mycenae.

Cretan types with the descending armed figure on the great signet-ring of Mycenae. In that case, as has been already pointed out,[1] the material form of the divinity is probably to be recognised in the double axe that fills the field between the descending warrior God and his seated consort. As already noted, the 'labrys' symbol of the Cretan and Carian Zeus, coupled with the sun and moon above, sufficiently define the character of the divine pair here represented. The poppies—emblem of sleep and the oriental *kéif*—held by the seated Goddess, were in later times generally an attribute of Demeter, but at Sikyon also of Aphroditê.[2] It has been already suggested that, whatever name may have originally belonged to the Goddess of the Mycenaean cult-scenes, whether in Cyprus or Greece proper, a part of her mythic being survived in that of the Goddess who in Crete is best known by her epithet, Ariadnê.[3]

---

[1] See above, p. 9 *seqq.*
[2] The Aphrodite of Kanachos at Sikyon held poppies in one hand and an apple in the

other, Paus. ii. 10, 5. Cf. Furtwängler, *Myk. Vasen*, p. 79, and *Antike Gemmen*, p. 36.
[3] Hesych. ἀδνόν, ἀγνόν, Κρῆτες. The form

On an electrum signet ring from a tomb of the Lower Town of Mycenae,[1] opened by Dr. Tsuntas in 1893, we may also with great probability recognise the same divine pair (Fig. 51). The Goddess is here seated with her back to a bush upon what may be variously interpreted as a simple seat or a small shrine. The male divinity here stands naked, except for his girdle and anklets, and armed with a spear or javelin. His left[2] forearm is bent forward and crosses that of the Goddess in the same position,[3] and the figures of both divinities express the same significant gesture in which a forefinger and thumb are pressed together. This is a very widespread expedient of sign-language for indicating agreement, and to the modern Neapolitan still conveys the idea of plighted troth.[4]

Two other signet rings remain to be described which afford some striking points of comparison with that from the Akropolis Treasure of

FIG. 52.—RELIGIOUS SCENE ON GOLD SIGNET RING FROM VAPHEIO TOMB (³⁄₂).

Mycenae. One of these (Fig. 52)[5] was found in the Vapheio tomb near Sparta. The other (Fig. 53)[6] was procured by Dr. Tsuntas in 1895 from a tomb in the lower town of Mycenae. Both designs present such an obvious parallelism in their general composition that they may best be described together.

On the Vapheio ring (Fig. 52) we see a female figure, here probably to be identified with the seated Goddess on Schliemann's ring, who stands beneath the overhanging branches of a fruit tree at the foot of which appears to be a stone pillar,[1] the reduplicated version of divinity. Rocks below. indicate that this is on a height, and a male figure, naked except for his sandals and gaiter-like foot gear and the usual loin-cloth and girdle, is seen in an energetic attitude either plucking the fruit for the Goddess from her own tree or pulling down the branch for her to gather it from. On Schliemann's ring a small female attendant behind the tree is seen engaged in plucking fruit for the same purpose.

On the recently discovered ring from Mycenae (Fig. 53) this part of the scene is reproduced with some variations in detail but with great general correspondence. The whole group is here placed on a stone base or terrace recalling that of the Knossian ring (Fig. 48), but here apparently of ruder and smaller masonry. Here a flounced figure answering apparently to the Goddess on the Vapheio ring stands with her hands drawn towards her waist.

FIG. 53.—RELIGIOUS SCENE ON GOLD SIGNET RING FROM MYCENAE (¾).

The broader features of sign-language are very universal in their application and in this case a common gesture for hunger among the American Indians may supply a useful parallel. It is made 'by passing the hands towards and backward from the sides of the body, denoting a gnawing sensation,'[2] and the pictograph for this sign curiously recalls the attitude of the figure on the ring. This explanation is quite appropriate to the subject. The Goddess here is seen looking towards the fruit-laden boughs of her sacred tree while a male attendant, in the same energetic attitude as the similar figure on the ring from Mycenae, hastens to satisfy her desire by pulling down a branch of

---

[1] This tree has been described by Tsuntas, 'Εφ. 'Αρχ., 1890, p. 170, as growing out of a large vessel (ὡσεὶ ἀπὸ ἀγγείου ἐπιμήκους ἐκφυόμενον), but a comparison with the parallel ring from Mycenae (Fig. 53) inclines me to believe that the object below, though certainly tub-like, is a somewhat thick column.

[2] Garrick Mallery, 'Pictographs of the North American Indians,' *Fourth Annual Report of the Bureau of Ethnology*, 1886, p. 236, and cf. Fig. 155, p. 235, representing the celebrated rock-painting on the Tule River, California.

the tree. The designs on both rings, which have been hitherto described as scenes of an orgiastic dance, are in fact full of meaning and depict an act of divine communion—the partaking by the Goddess of the fruit of her sacred tree. In this case as in the other the tree is in immediate association with a sacred pillar, here seen in its shrine. The tree seems to spread from the top of a small sanctuary raised on a high base and displaying an entablature supported by two columns, in the opening between which, but not reaching as far as the impost, is seen the pillar form of the divinity. Probably as in the case of the Knossian ring which supplies a somewhat similar effect the tree must really be regarded as also standing within the shrine or *temenos*.

In the field above to the right of the central figure on the Vapheio ring, together with two uncertain objects, one of which may be a spray or an ear of barley, there appears a device of symbolic significance.

This object (Fig. 54, 5) is described by Dr. Tsuntas as a cross-like axe with two appendages while Dr. Max Meyer speaks of it simply as a double-axe.[1] It will, however, be observed that the lower extremity terminates in

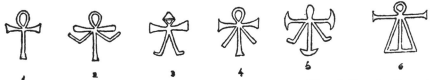

FIG. 54.—SYMBOLS DERIVED FROM THE EGYPTIAN *Ankh*. 1. The *Ankh*. 2. Two-armed Egyptian Form. 3 and 4. Hittite Types. 5. From Mycenaean Ring. 6. On Carthaginian Stele.

the same way as the two side limbs and that in neither case is there any true delineation of an axe—though the curving edges may not improbably be due to some cross influence from the double-axe symbol.

For the true meaning and derivation of the present figure we must look on the Hittite side. It is in fact unquestionably allied to a modification of the Egyptian *Ankh* or symbol of life and divinity (Fig. 54, 1) which effected itself in the 'Hittite' regions of Anatolia and Northern Syria. Already on a cylinder of rather early Chaldaean type, but probably belonging to that region, the *Ankh* is seen in its Egyptian form as a symbol of divinity behind the hand of a seated God.[2] Somewhat later it becomes of frequent occurrence in cult-scenes and is also an accompaniment of Hittite princes.[3] Already in some versions of the *Ankh* belonging to the earliest dynasties of Egypt, it appears with a divided stem below.[4] In accordance with a well-known tendency of Hittite art, whether or not with a reminiscence of this very

[1] *Jahrbuch d. k. d. Inst.* 7 (1892), p. 191. So too Fritze, *op. cit.*

[2] Lajarde, *Culte de Mithra*, Pl. XXXVI. Fig. 13.

[3] Cf. Lajarde, *op. cit.* Pl. XXXIV. Fig. 6;

Pl. XXXV. Figs. 2 and 4; Pl. XXXVI. Figs. 8, 9, 10 and 11.

[4] On objects belonging to the first Dynasties found by M. Amélineau at Abydos.

early Egyptian tradition, the symbol now shows a tendency to acquire two legs and even at times a head. On the Tarsus seal[1] it appears above an altar and associated with other ritual scenes, in slightly variant forms in which the lower limb has divided into two legs and the circle at the top has sometimes a kind of conical cap (see Fig. 54, 3). On a cylinder[2] it is seen in the hands of an attendant behind a princely worshipper in a form which combines the two legs with the original lower limb (Fig. 54, 4). It will be sufficient to compare this last modification with those on the Tarsus seal to see that in the Mycenaean figure we have to do with another member of the same series. In other words the Mycenaean symbol is a direct derivative from the Egyptian *ankh*, as a sign of divinity, through intermediate forms which must be sought in the cycle of Hittite iconography. This symbol both on the Tarsus and Indilimma seals is placed in juxtaposition with a triangular sign probably denoting a Goddess and must itself be taken to represent the male member of a divine pair. The allied form (Fig. 54, 6) was copied by me from a stele at Carthage, and was surmounted by the orb and crescent of two conjoined divinities.

In the present case the curved ends of three of the limbs suggest as already noted that this ancient symbol has been crossed by that of the double axe, and its substitution in the place of the axe and armed figure on the ring from the Mycenae treasure seems to show that it stands here in connexion with the same God. It may therefore have a direct bearing on the subject immediately below it.

The discoverer of the Vapheio ring failed to recognise the character of the representation on this side of the field and even described it as ' an object like an insect, but of disproportionate size.'[3] Max Mayer, Furtwängler, H. von Fritze and others have since seen in it a helmet with a long crest resting on a shield. A close examination had long convinced me that the representation in question really consisted of a small female figure in the usual flounced dress, with one arm bent under her and the other stretched forward, prostrate on a large Mycenaean shield. On the more recently discovered ring from Mycenae we now see a different version of the same scene. A female figure in the habitual costume this time leans forward resting her two arms in a pensive attitude on the balustrade of what appears

---

[1] Cf. Thomas Tyler, *Babylonian and Oriental Record*, 1887, pp. 150, 151, and ' The Nature of Hittite Writing,' *Trans. Congress of Orientalists*, London, 1892, p. 261 *seqq.* As Tyler rightly points out, this development of the symbol stands in a near relation to the ' headed triangle' emblem of Baal and Ashtoreth on Carthaginian stelae. Here the side limbs assume the form of arms and this anthropomorphised symbol seems to have affected the later development of the sacred cone at Paphos and elsewhere. The distinguishing feature of the Carthaginian modifi-

cation of the Ankh is the arms, in the Hittite the legs.

[2] Lajarde, *op. cit.* Pl. XVIII. Fig. 7.

[3] Tsuntas, 'Εφ. 'Αρχ. 1890, p. 170 ' ἀντικείμενόν τι ὡσεὶ ἔντομον ὑπερμέγεθες.' Max Mayer (*Jahrbuch d. Arch. Inst.* 1892, p. 189), recognised the shield but took the figure above it for a helmet with a high crest. He regards the shield and the imaginary helmet as having been laid aside by the male figure. But the analogy of the parallel ring Fig. 53 shows that the figure is simply an attendant.

to be a small columnar shrine like that which encloses the sacred tree and pillar on the opposite side of the field. With down-turned face, she seems to contemplate the contents of this little sanctuary, which is divided by a central column into two compartments. The first of these, hung with two festoons, contains a short baetylic pillar like that on the analogous ring from Vapheio. In the second is what on minute examination appears to be a miniature but clearly defined Mycenaean shield. Here then with additional accompaniments we find the theme of the outermost design of the Vapheio ring also reproduced on the example from Mycenae. In one case we see a female devotee actually prostrate on the shield, in the other she bends down over it leaning for support on the small shrine in which it seems to be hung. The same parallelism thus runs through all the leading features of the two rings.

It is true that in the last pair of scenes on the extreme right of the field there is a great difference in the size of the body-shields. But this disproportion is really conditioned by the character of the two representations. In the one case we have only to do with the shield itself and the recumbent votary. In the other, the female figure leans on a shrine containing the shield, and the size of the shield itself is naturally reduced. The shrine itself, we may imagine, was really much larger in proportion to the leaning figure, and the whole composition is analogous to others of the same glyptic cycle in which, as in the ring shown in Fig. 64, the seated Goddess is seen seated against the shrine containing her aniconic image, or, as in the case of Cypriote cylinders, using the sanctuary itself as a throne. It does not necessarily follow from this that the shrine itself was quite so diminutive.

The scene to the right of the first ring, the female figure prostrate on the body-shield, is evidently one of mourning for a dead warrior. We recall the large body-shield covering the body of the slain combatant beneath the horses of the chariot on the funeral stela of Mycenae, though in the present case no human figure is visible. The shield by itself, however, is sufficiently suggestive of departed valour, and at Falerii we find the early Italian oval shield, afterwards imitated by the Gauls, supplying, as laid on its back, the model for a sepulchral monument. It has already been suggested above,[1] that the shield equally with the double axe may be regarded as the material impersonation of the divinity. The *ancile* fallen from heaven, which represents the Mycenaean shield on Italian soil, recalls the sky-fallen baetylic stone.

There are, however, indications that the mourning scene on the ring does not refer to the decease of a human warrior. The emblem of male divinity above must reasonably be taken in connexion with it. Moreover, on Schliemann's ring from the Akropolis treasure at Mycenae, and again on the painted slab, the Mycenaean body-shield appears as a prominent attribute of a warrior God, whose character in the case of the ring is further indicated by the double axe.

The religious intent of the representation is further brought out by the

---

[1] See p. 24.

companion scene on the more recently discovered ring.   The shrine, in which the shield is here apparently hung up, and the baetylic column contained in it, gives the whole an aspect of consecration.   At the same time, the attitude of the female figure leaning on the balustrade, like that of the votary prone on the shield itself on the other signet, is strongly suggestive of mourning. The baetylic column, as has been already shown, can be also a sepulchral monument, not necessarily of a human divinity.   We seem to be in the presence of the tomb of a divine hero, or rather of a warrior God.

We have already ventured to detect one surviving offshoot of the cult of an armed Mycenaean divinity in that of the Amyklaean Apollo, common both to Cyprus and Laconia, and the affiliation with Apollo in another form is brought out by the persistence of the primitive aniconic image in the case of Apollo Agyieus.   On the other hand, the spear is also an early attribute of Zeus, and, as already pointed out, the double-axe, or *labrys*, on the ring from the Mycenae Treasure, brings the male divinity into a close relationship with the Zeus Labrandeus of Karia, and the Zeus-Minôs of the Cretan Labyrinth.   At Knossos, his aspect as a solar deity, so well illustrated by the gold ring from that site, is brought out by his connexion with Pasiphaê, the Moon Goddess.   Elsewhere, as at Gortyna, we see the Cretan Zeus associated with Europa, the daughter of Telephassa, another form of the Moon Goddess.

But this identification of the armed divinity of this dual cult, or whom the Mycenaean body-shield might be regarded as a special attribute, with the 'Cretan Zeus' of later religious tradition, supplies an interesting commentary on what appears to be the sepulchral shrine and suspended shield on our ring.   We have here, it may be, a prehistoric representation of the 'Tomb of Zeus.'

§ 26.—*Sacral Gateways or Portal Shrines, mostly associated with Sacred Trees.*

The sanctity of the portal or doorway in primitive cult is very general,[1] and its association with the sacred tree is well brought out by some of the Pompeian wall-paintings.   To this day the traveller in the Caucasus may see outside the Ossete houses a rude arch or gateway placed beside the stump which represents the ancestral tree of the household.   In Phrygia we have a series of inscriptions coupling the altar (βωμός) and doorway (θύρα), as sacral erections.   The doorway itself, like the dolmen in parts of India, can, as much as the baetylic pillar, serve as the temporary dwelling place of the God or Spirit and, in a sense, as his material image.

In the gold ring (Fig. 55) from the Lower Town of Mycenae, a man in the usual Mycenaean garb, who perhaps answers to the male attendant of the Goddess in other religious scenes, is seen reaching out his hand towards the

---

[1] For the triliths of primitive cult we need go no further than Stonehenge.

topmost bough of what is perhaps also intended for a fruit tree. Behind him with the branches of another tree visible above the back, stands a large *agrimi* or Cretan wild goat—an animal seen elsewhere in connexion with female votaries. This goat may represent the sacred animal of either the male or female member of the divine pair referred to in the preceding sections. As an attribute of Aphroditê it is well known in later cult; on the other hand the votive remains of the Diktaean Cave as well as the traditions of

FIG. 55.—PORTAL SHRINE ON GOLD SIGNET RING FROM MYCENAE (⅔).

Amaltheia tend to show that this animal was sacred to the indigenous 'Zeus' at an earlier period than the bull. The ox indeed in any form seems to be absent in the more primitive archaeological strata of the island. Though frequent in representations of the Mycenaean period, among the earlier Cretan pictographic figures it is entirely non-apparent.

The 'portal shrine' here seems to be supported on either side by double columns. The same type of shrine recurs on an unpublished gold ring from Mycenae (Fig. 56).[1] Here we see a female votary standing in a half facing attitude between a tri-foliate tree or group of three trees —for the trunk too seems to be triply divided—and a small shrine on a rocky knoll. The sprays of some smaller plants rise on each side of her, and two longer shoots form a kind of canopy over the tree and the standing figure. The votary herself wears the usual Mycenaean dress and the long plaits of her hair stream down beneath her right arm, the upper part of which is encircled with a ring. Her feet point in the direction of the tree, but her

FIG. 56.—CULT SCENE WITH SACRED TREE AND PORTAL ON GOLD SIGNET RING, MYCENAE (⅔).

---

[1] In my own collection

head and the upper part of her body are turned backwards, so that she gazes on the rock shrine, towards which, moreover, her right hand is raised in the attitude of adoration.

The shrine itself consists of what are apparently two pairs of slender pillars supporting an entablature consisting of three members—an architrave, a frieze with vertical lines, which seem to represent the continuation of the lines of the columns below, and a wider cornice above. The whole forms a kind of archway, and between the double columns is visible a small object which has the appearance of a flying bird. Resting on the entablature is seen one of the usual two-horned appendages of Mycenaean cult, from behind which rises a spray. Two other small sprays shoot from the rocks immediately on either side of the shrine. These connecting sprays and the divided attitude of the Goddess link together the sanctity of the triple tree and the shrine.

On another signet ring of gold found by Dr. Tsuntas, in 1895, in a tomb of the Lower Town of Mycenae,[1] occurs a cult-scene, somewhat enigmatic in its details, which requires careful analysis (Fig. 57). Two female

FIG. 57.—CULT SCENE WITH SACRED TREE AND PORTAL; GOLD SIGNET RING, MYCENAE (⅔).

votaries of the usual type stand on a stone terrace, on either side of a central tree shrine, which is raised on a graduated base. The summit sanctuary consists of a group of the three trees, the heads of which appear above, and the trunks within an arch, which consists of an entablature supported by two pillars built of a series of separate blocks. From the centre of this, a line of dots, perhaps representing a path—the *via sacra* to the shrine—descends to the terrace below. At this point, on either side, are what appear to be two doors, with an interval between, as if they had been thrown open, and somewhat recalling the Gates of Heaven, opened wide by the attendant genii for the passage of Samas, as seen on Chaldaean cylinders. We may, perhaps, suppose that the whole represents a shrine on a peak surrounded by a temenos

---

[1] I also owe the impression from which Fig. 57 has been drawn to Dr. Tsuntas's kindness. The signet has since been figured by Furtwängler, *Ant. Gemmen.* ii. p. 24, and by H. von Fritze, *op. cit.* p. 73, 5.

wall, which is here made to descend in regular steps. On the lower step of this is seen, on either side, a cypress-like tree, and a tree of the same kind may be recognised behind the adorant to the right, surrounded with a dotted oval, which, perhaps, may be taken to indicate a kind of sacred halo like that round the Cypriote obelisks and pillars. Behind the other female worshipper is a bush-covered rock.

Attention has already been called to the significance of the tree trinity in the central sanctuary of this design, which also seems to find a parallel in the last described signet ring.

An illustration of a holy gateway or shrine without a sacred tree is supplied by a gold-plated silver ring (Fig. 58),[1] found by Dr. Tsuntas, in a tomb of the lower town of Mycenae in 1893. The lower part of the bezel has unfortunately perished, but the remaining half shows the upper parts of the bodies of three female votaries, the middle one of whom

FIG. 58.—SACRAL GATEWAY AND VOTARIES ON GOLD-PLATED SILVER RING, MYCENAE (⅘).

raises her hand in the attitude of adoration before two upright double columns, supporting a kind of double impost or lintel upon which, as a sign of its sanctity, rests the cult object, already referred to as 'the horns of consecration.'

On a steatite bead seal of somewhat rude execution, found in a Mycenaean beehive tomb at Ligortino, in Crete, there occurs a somewhat variant design (Fig. 59).[2] The doorway here seems to belong to a kind of temenos, analogous on a smaller scale to that of Fig. 48 above, within which the tree perhaps rose on an elevation. The tree itself seems to be surrounded by a small inner fence, just as the sacred cone on the coins of Byblos appears in a lattice-work

---

[1] From an impression taken with Dr. Tsuntas's kind permission. The signet is also reproduced by Furtwängler, *Ant. Gemmen*, Pl. VI. 4, and by H. von Fritze, *Strena Helbigiana*, p. 72, 4.

[2] The greater part of the contents of this tomb were acquired by the Louvre; unfortunately, however, the lentoid intaglio in question is wanting. Fig. 59 above is from a sketch of the stone made by me when it was in the finder's possession shortly after the discovery of the tomb.

enclosure within the great court of the temenos.   Behind this rises a horned prominence which either represents a part of the usual two-horned cult object or a single horn having the same sacral import.   It supplies an interesting parallel to the single horn on the capstone of the cellular shrine, to be described in the next section, the misinterpretation of which as the back of a throne led Dr Reichel so far astray.[1]

A female votary stands before the enclosure with the hand raised in the usual attitude of adoration.   But the most significant feature of the design remains to be described.   Behind the doorway and beneath the platform on which the tree rests is engraved a large crescent which clearly connects this cult scene with a lunar divinity.   The position of this crescent, which appa-

FIG. 59.—SACRED TREE AND ENCLOSURE ON STEATITE LENTOID, LIGORTINO, CRETE (¾).

rently brings it into relation with a sanctuary below this, suggests the explanation that the gateway and outer temenos may have led to the mouth of a cave sacred to the Moon Goddess, above which again was a holy tree.

§ 27.—*The Dolmen Shrines of Primitive Cult and Dove Shrines of Mycenae.*

It is possible that some of the objects described in the preceding section as sacral doorways or portal shrines really represent slabs supported by four pillars, and that we have here to do with holy 'table-stones,' or to adopt the well-known Celtic word for this religious structure, with 'dolmens.'   The double pillars on either side of some of the examples given might bear out

---

[1] See below p. 91.

this idea, but on the other hand the elaborate entablature of two stages, which they support, weighs in favour of the sacral gateway.

In considering the pillar cult of the Mycenaeans we are continually brought face to face with an aspect of this ancient worship, which can never be lost sight of—its connexion namely with the monumental forms of primitive sepulchral ritual. In India, where a living study can be made of this baetylic cult, it is seen at every turn to be deep-rooted in sepulchral religion. The stone chamber of the grave mound can itself be regarded as the dwelling-place of a Spirit, and receive worship as a divinity. At other times it is dissociated from direct sepulchral contact, and becomes a miniature shrine for a small pillar idol. Good examples of a dolmen shrine of this kind placed at the foot of sacred trees may still be seen in the Shiarai Hills between Madras and Malabar,[1] of which one is reproduced for comparison in Fig. 60. Here we see the rude baetylic pillar surrounded by smaller pebbles, set up on the floor of the

FIG. 60.—BAETYLIC STONE IN DOLMEN SHRINE, SHIARAI HILLS, INDIA.

megalithic cell in a manner which recalls the small pillars seen within the shrines in some of the Mycenaean cult scenes described above.

In other cases it will be seen that the baetylic pillar itself performs a structural function and helps to support the capstone of its dolmen shrine.

The Mycenaean column in its developed architectural form, as can be seen from its entablature, essentially belongs to woodwork structure. The fundamental idea of its sanctity as a ' pillar of the house,' may at times, as in the instances quoted above,[2] have been derived from the original sanctity of the tree trunk whence it was hewn, and a form, in this way possessing religious associations, have been taken over into stone-work. But there is also what seems to be conclusive evidence that among the Mycenaeans pillar supports of a very primitive form of stone construction have left their trace on the Mycenaean column in its perfected shape, and explain indeed its most characteristic feature, namely the downward tapering outline which

[1] M. J. Wallhouse, 'Non-Sepulchral Rude Stone Monuments,' *Journ. Anthr. Inst.* vii. p. 21 *seqq.*

[2] See p. 47.

distinguishes it alike from the columns of Egypt and the East, and from those of later Greece.

There exists a well-marked type of primitive and originally sepulchral structures, consisting of megalithic blocks, in which, in addition to the massive side walls, stone pillars are also introduced into the dolmen chamber to give a central support to the roof slabs.

This form of construction seems to be quite typical in the Iberic West. In some of the great Spanish megalithic structures, like that of Antequera, stone pillars are seen at intervals along the centre of the gallery which serve as central supports for its great capping slabs, the ends of which rest on the upright blocks that form the side-walls. In more than one type of pre-historic buildings found in the Balearic islands a similar structural method presents itself (Figs. 61, 62)[1] The centre of a horizontally vaulted chamber

FIG. 61.—PILLARED CHAMBER OF 'NAU,' MINORCA.

derives its support from a column the upper part of which consists of cross slabs gradually increasing in size so as to present the appearance of a gradually widening pillar and capital. The object of this is to meet the inwardly inclining walls of the chamber and form a kind of Tirynthian passage all round. It will be seen that in its most characteristic development this class of pillar supplies a simple explanation for the origin of the peculiar downward taper of the Mycenaean column. This is the true 'Pillar of the House.'

In many caves, however, the Balearic monuments, and notably the so-called Talyots, show an upright block with almost perpendicular sides, on the top of which one or more 'capital' slabs are laid. Several pillars of this kind which are in fact huge biliths have survived, while the walls of the surrounding

---

[1] Cartailhac, *Monuments Primiti s des îles Baléares.* Fig. 61 is taken from a monument of the kind known as '*Nau*' (*op. cit.* Pl. 46), Fig. 62 from an underground chamber of the kind known as '*Cova*' (*op. cit.* p. 18).

chamber built of smaller blocks have been entirely ruined, and they are popularly known as 'altars' in the island. The buildings in which they originally stood do not seem to have been ordinary dwelling houses since, as M. Cartailhac has pointed out, only a single structure of this kind is to be found in each of the prehistoric settlements of Minorca. It is possible therefore that they were shrines, and in that case the so-called 'altars' may well have been regarded like the Mycenaean and Semitic 'pillars of the house' as the seat of the tutelary divinity. Many of the Bhuta stones of India, already referred to as baetylic forms of a spiritual being, consist of an upright pillar with a cross piece at the top which seems to have been derived from some such primitive structure as the preceding.

We shall see the same type of primitive pillar as that of the Balearic islands, tapering towards the base and with capping stones above, in the side cells of the great megalithic buildings of the Maltese islands, which are

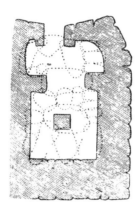

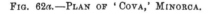

FIG. 62*a*.—PLAN OF 'COVA,' MINORCA.　　　FIG. 62*b*.—SECTION OF 'COVA,' MINORCA.

certainly connected with a primitive sepulchral cult.[1] It is moreover a noteworthy fact that the front outlines of the supporting walls of some of the sepulchral cells of the period immediately preceding that of Mycenae recently discovered at Chalandrianê in Syra present the appearance of similar columns gradually decreasing towards the base.[2]

The dolmen-like character of many of the Mycenaean shrines upon the rings, and the reminiscences they present of such primitive forms as the trilith in connexion with the sacred tree much as we see it on the Pompeian frescoes, make it natural to turn to the same class of primitive structures for further comparisons. When, then, upon two of the gold signet rings,[3] we see through the simple trilithic opening of a small shrine a pillar with flat capping stones

---

[1] See below, p. 99.

[2] 'Εφ. 'Αρχ. 1899, Pl. VII. 4. See above, p. 22.

[3] See below, Figs. 63, 64. These designs

have been already independently compared by Max. Mayer, 'Myk. Beitr.' ii. *Jahrbuch*, 1893, p. 190, 5.

laid on it capital-wise standing beneath the middle of the lintel or roof stone there can be no reasonable doubt that we have to do with a survival—modified no doubt in several ways—of the same kind of columnar cell that we see in the Talyots and other similar structures.

A good example of the cellular shrine, the lintel of which is supported by a pillar with capping stones increasing in size, will be seen in Fig. 63 from a gold ring from Mycenae.[1] Here we see the baetylic shrine approached by three female votaries with one hand raised in the gesture of adoration, two of whom hold sprays taken, no doubt, from a sacred tree. Upon the top of the shrine, as in so many parallel cases, appears the symbol of consecration with which we are already familiar, except that in this case as in Fig. 59 above only a single horn is represented. This omission is, perhaps, due in both cases to the fact that while the votary faces the two-horned object, the spectator may be supposed to see it in profile. In the present instance, however, as what appears to be the base of the object in question is apparently visible, the second horn may have been simply left out owing to the fact that the votary's forearm intrudes into the space it might otherwise have occupied.

FIG. 63.—FEMALE VOTARIES BEFORE PILLAR SHRINE; GOLD SIGNET RING, MYCENAE ($\frac{3}{1}$).

The character of the worship and of the objects represented is abundantly clear from the examples already reproduced. Yet the comparative materials at his disposal did not save Dr. Reichel from a capital error in describing the cult scene on this ring.

The ingenious author of 'pre-Hellenic cults' has taken the remaining horn of the 'horns of consecration' for the back of a seat and the base for its arm. The double-outlined side blocks of the shrine become four legs naively represented with the further pair just seen inside the nearer, and the baetylic pillar becomes a fifth leg or central prop, a little superfluous, it might be thought, for an incorporeal sitter. For the whole, according to Dr. Reichel's theory, is a throne of a Mycenaean divinity who is himself invisible to his worshippers.[2]

Upon this strangely fantastic base, for there is no other, has

[1] Tsuntas, Μυκῆναι, Pl. V. 3 ; Perrot et Chipiez, vi. Fig. 428, 23. Reichel, *Vorhellenische Götterkulte*, p. 3 ; Furtwängler, *Ant. Gemmen*, iii. p. 44, Fig. 21. H. von Fritze, *Strena Helbigiana*, p. 73, 3.

[2] W. Reichel, *Ueber vorhellenische Götterkulte*, p. 5 : 'Das Gebäude ist ganz deutlich ein *Thron*. Vier Beine die naiv so gezeichnet sind dass man das jenseitige Paar innerhalb des vorderen erkennt, zusammt einer Säule, tragen das Sitzbrett : über diesem eine niedere Armlehne und eine steile Rückenlehne, streng in Profil.'

been built up the whole theory of a Mycenaean cult of Sacred Thrones. All that has been said in these pages is certainly in favour of the view that the cult objects of the Mycenaeans were of the aniconic class. The thing actually worshipped was the tree or pillar possessed by the divinity. But, as pointed out above in the case of the pictorial representations seen on the signet rings, the anthropomorphic figures of divinities are introduced beside their aniconic equivalents. Sometimes the divinity is placed beneath the sacred tree. On the fellow ring to that on which this theory of throne-cult has been based, the Goddess sits beside her shrine. On a Cypro-Mycenaean cylinder she sits upon it. Were the present representation a throne we should expect to see, as in fact we find on another signet, the divinity upon it.[1] But in truth the idea of a divine throne belongs to a period of more advanced anthropomorphic cult. The ideas that underly the cult of baetylic stones and sacred trees show that these material objects did not so much

FIG 64.—GODDESS SEATED BEFORE PILLAR SHRINE, ON GOLD SIGNET RING, MYCENAE (¾).

serve as a resting place for airy spiritual forms, but themselves absorbed and incorporated their essence; they are ἔμψυχοι λίθοι. As the idea of the visible anthropomorphic divinity encroaches on the earlier notions, it is these pre-existing baetylic shapes that serve at first as seats and supports for it. Among these the throne has no place. It is rather the omphalos, the altar, the tomb, or the shrine itself, that became the seat.

A gold signet-ring now in the Berlin Museum (Fig. 64) gives a variant form of the same design as the above. In this case the pillar shrine is raised on a kind of base and the Goddess herself sits with her back against it, holding up a mirror-like object and receiving the adoration of a female votary. Here we are left in no doubt as to the sacred character of the sup-

---

[1] See the signet ring, Fig. 51 above.

porting pillar within the cell, for at its foot the familiar 'horns of conse-cration' stand clearly defined.

These single baetylic cells with the sacred object at the foot of the pillar. or upon the roof-stone lead us naturally to what is really only a more elaborate example of the same religious structures—namely the triple sanctuaries with the doves, of which models in thin gold plate were found in the third Akropolis grave at Mycenae (Fig. 65). The building here is more elaborate and conventionalised. Like the small Phoenician shrine known as the Maabed of Amrit the actual cells are raised upon a stonework base and a Mycenaean altar is set on the roof of the central shrine. But the objects which the sanctuary itself was intended to enshrine are the same baetylic 'pillars of the house,' having, as in the last example, the 'horns of conse-cration set at the foot of each. They seem to stand at least a little way

FIG. 65.—GOLD SHRINE WITH DOVES; THIRD AKROPOLIS GRAVE, MYCENAE.
(From Schliemann's 'Mycenae.')

back from the openings themselves, since there is room for the cult object to be placed in front of them.

The parallelism between the triple dove shrines and the single baetylic cells on the rings must set all doubts at rest as to the true character of the miniature temples with which we have to deal. How far astray the ingenuity of commentators could go in the absence of comparative materials is shown by the theory which saw in the dove shrine the front of a large basilican building and in the Mycenaean altar of the ordinary type, which crowns the central cell, a window with 'semicircles introduced either to fill up the space or as ornaments on the shutters.'[1]

---

[1] Schuchhardt (Sellers' Translation), p. 200. 'The curved lines under the columns of the niches should be interpreted in the same manner : they merely cover the empty space

It has been already noticed that the comparative size of the doves on the gold shrines and of the 'horns of consecration' both on these and the analogous pillar-cells upon the rings, are themselves indications that we have here to do with quite small structures. We see before us, in fact, cellular chapels which still bear traces of their origin from the simple structural forms akin to the pillared galleries of Spain or the primitive monuments of the Balearic islands. This kind of baetylic cell is not by any means always of the type in which the pillar acts, as in the above instances, as a support for the roof-stones. Sometimes, as has been already pointed out, we see a short upright stone, the top of which stands well below the roof slab. But in all cases it is safe to say that we have to do with comparatively small cells.

§ 28.—*Fresco representing a small Baetylic Temple from the Palace at Knossos.*

The dove shrines of Mycenae though still small in dimensions are already considerably advanced beyond what has been described above as the primitive dolmen cell. It has been reserved, however, for the Palace of Knossos to produce the evidence of a still further development of a similar type of Mycenaean sanctuary.

This is supplied by some fragments of fresco, part of a series in a curious miniature style, found in a room to the north of the great Eastern Court of the Palace. The associated fragments show large crowds of people of both sexes, groups of elaborately dressed Mycenaean ladies engaged in animated conversation, warriors armed with spears and javelins, part of the city walls and the other buildings. A fragment of the wall of a sanctuary belonging to this series with a row of 'horns of consecration' on the top, has been already given in Fig. 18.[1] A coloured reproduction of the pieces of fresco representing the Mycenaean shrine will be seen on Plate V.

The open space in front of this small temple is crowded with men and women, the sexes being distinguished according to the Egyptian convention by their being respectively coloured reddish brown and white. To facilitate this effect the artist has availed himself of a kind of pictorial shorthand, giving the outlines of the men on a red ground and of the women on a white. A seated female figure is also depicted with her back to the right outer wall of the shrine itself, a useful indication of its comparative dimensions.

The small temple here delineated is essentially an outgrowth of the same type as that of the dove-shrines. As to the question whether it, too, had an altar on the roof we have no evidence, but otherwise the fresco has preserved enough of its construction to enable us to reconstitute the façade

or else they are patterns decorating the doors.' Still, Dr. Schuchhardt admitted 'the position of the columns themselves in the centre of the openings remains a problem.'

[1] P. 38.

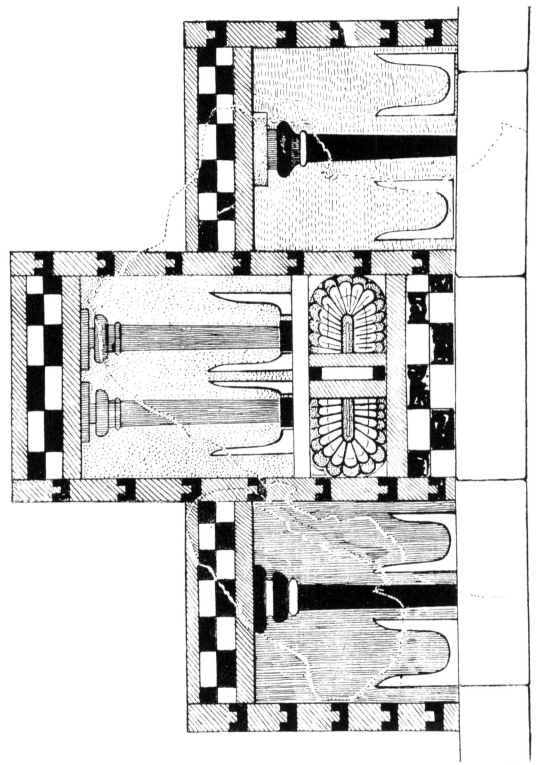

FIG. 66.—FAÇADE OF SMALL MYCENAEAN TEMPLE, COMPLETED FROM THE FRESCO PAINTING OF THE PALACE, KNOSSOS.

H

in its entirety (Fig. 66). The building rests on a·base consisting of large white blocks, which apparently continue beyond it. As to the character of these the existing remains of the Palace supply a sufficient indication. They are the great gypsum blocks, such as in large parts of the building, and notably along its western side, form the lower part of the walls, which above this massive layer seem largely to have consisted of clay strengthened by a wooden framework, and coated with plaster often brilliantly painted with polychrome designs. Analogy, as well as the varied colouring on the face of the building, would lead us to suppose that the same structural method had also been largely resorted to in the shrine reproduced in the fresco. The mortise and tenon motive of the upright posts which divide the cells and mark the outer walls of the building are certainly taken from woodwork, and seem to imply a succession of vertical and horizontal beams.

There can, of course, be no doubt that the white and black chequer-work is taken from stone-work construction, though the builders of the Palace—who were surprisingly modern in some of their procedures—were quite capable of producing stucco imitation of masonry. In the south-west porch of the building is a clay and rubble wall faced with painted plaster, the lower part of which imitates blocks of variously coloured marble. As in the case of the Temple this chequer work is apparently contained in a wooden framework, it is safer to regard it too as painted plaster. The white and black chequering is a favourite decoration of Egyptian architectural painting,[1] and it is probable that this feature, as undoubtedly a characteristic detail, to be noticed below, in the formation of the capitals of the columns, was borrowed from this source.

Of peculiar interest is the appearance, immediately below the central opening, of two elongated half rosettes, separated by a threefold division, which present a most striking analogy to the frieze[2] found in the vestibule of the Palace at Tiryns. The white and the blue of the side slabs here answer to the alabaster material and blue glass (κύανος χυτός) inlaying of the Tirynthian example, while the red streaks show that the half rosettes were in this case still further coloured. The parallelism here is of such a kind as to induce the belief that what is seen on the façade of the Knossian shrine also represents actual slabs of inlaid alabaster. But there is a further detail in the present case which confirms the conclusion that these are not merely spaces filled with painted stucco. The alabaster slabs, with the similar foliated designs, from the Palace of Tiryns are linked by smaller pieces in the same material, the threefold division of which has been recognised as supplying the prototype of the Doric triglyph.[3] These Mycenaean triglyphs stand forward somewhat beyond the plane of the 'metopes,' and secure them by overlapping their edges. At Tiryns the triglyphs are of alabaster, like the intervening slabs. But on the Knossian shrine the outer posts of these,

---

[1] Compare for instance the chequer decoration over a house from a Sixth Dynasty Tomb. (Maspero, *Man. of Egypt. Arch.*, Engl. Edition, p. 21).

[2] See Dörpfeld in Schliemann's *Tiryns*, p.

284 *seqq.* and Pl. IV. and Perrot et Chipiez *L'Art*, etc. vi. p. 698 *seqq.*

[3] Dörpfeld, in Schliemann's *Tiryns*, p. 284. Perrot et Chipiez, *L'Art*, etc., vi. p. 710 *seqq.*

as well as those beneath the metopes, are coloured with the same brown hue as the pillars on either side of them—in other words, they are of wood-work. It is evident that this is the earlier form, and that the original Mycenaean triglyph that supplied the prototype for the Doric, was of the same material as the guttae below them, which are well known to be the translation into stone of wooden rivets. Here, in fact, we have wood-work bars so fitted as to lock the edges of two alabaster plaques. Had the 'metope' fields been of plaster there would have been no occasion for a separate wooden triglyph.

The white horizontal coping immediately above the triglyph and metopes, on which the bases of the uppermost pairs of columns rest, is probably of gypsum, like the larger blocks of the plinth below, from which the columns of the side chapels rise.

The columns themselves, of which there are a pair in the central shrine, and one in each of the wings, are undoubtedly of wood. Except for some square pillars made of separate blocks, no trace of stone shafts or capitals was found in the Palace of Knossos, and their non-discovery is quite in keeping with the evidence supplied by the Palaces of Tiryns [1] and Mycenae. At Knossos, however, we have the positive phenomenon that the burnt remains of wooden shafts of columns resting on the stone disks that formed their bases were actually found in the Throne Room of the Palace. These columns, three in number, which supported the roof of the small *impluvium*, were of cypress wood, a material which seems to have been commonly used here, as in the Palace of Odysseus.[2]

It is possible that those in the wings of the present design, the shafts of which are coloured black, were of different materials from the central pair, which are brown, though of a somewhat redder hue than the woodwork of the front of the building. But the variations in hue—especially noteworthy in the capital of the right-hand column—where blue, reddish-brown, black and white succeed one another—show that whatever the underlying material the surface of the wood was painted over.

Certain black markings on the echinus of the capital above referred to perhaps indicate the existence of a fluted foliation like that of the half capital from the 'Treasury of Atreus,' which also recurs in the metopes already described. Both this foliation, and the inlaid work that goes with it, are derived from contemporary Egypt, as may be seen from the fragments of capitals from the Palace of Akhenaten, at Tell-el-Amarna. Another feature of these capitals is equally Egyptian. This is the small rectangular cushion which intervenes between the rest of the capital and the slab, suggestive of a beam-end upon which the architrave immediately rests.

On the other hand, the shafts of the columns have the downward taper characteristic of the Mycenaean order. This, it may be noted, is specially appropriate in a building which *ex hypothesi* represents the translation of the primitive stone cells with their Talyot-like supporting pillars into a more roomy structure, the framework of which is of wood.

---

[1] See Dörpfeld in Schliemann's *Tiryns*, p. 270 *seqq*.   [2] Homer, *Od.* xvii. 340.

H 2

Here, too, as in the case of the dove shrines, and the smaller baetylic cells already described, the sacred character of the pillars is indicated by the horns in front of them, and beside them. The clear way in which this cult object is indicated in the fresco before us, must, in fact, remove all remaining doubt as to the true meaning of the curved design at the foot of the pillars of the dove shrines and the so-called altars of the signet rings which has been so variously explained. The columns of the Knossian shrine apparently approach the outer edge of the openings, leaving room, however, in front of them for the ' horns of consecration.'

The word cell, or chapel, has been used to express the three compartments of the sanctuary, for it is impossible to regard it merely as a triple archway open to the day. Had this been the case the ground colour seen through each opening would have been the same. But, as a matter of fact, the background of these is painted successively a reddish-brown, azure blue, and yellow. They must be regarded, therefore, as closed chambers. The evidence before us, moreover, leads to the conclusion that the whole structure, though somewhat larger than the dove shrines, is still of small dimensions. The horned objects are in height over a third that of the columns. The heads of the crowd in the space in front of the building, and still more the female figure seated with her back to the right wall, afford a still nearer guide to the size of the whole. If the building is proportionately rendered, it would appear that the height of its central part from the ground level to the summit was not more than nine feet.

§ 29.—*Parallels to the Baetylic Shrines of the Mycenaeans, supplied by the Megalithic Sanctuaries of the Maltese Islands.*

From the evidence already put together it will be seen that the Mycenaean cult of trees and pillars, in common with the whole Mycenaean civilisation, must be regarded as *in situ* in its Aegean homes. It fits on to a parallel system of primitive worship on the Anatolian and Syrian side. In its external aspects it shows signs of adaptation from Egyptian, to a less extent from Semitic sources, and it has also been possible to cite a striking analogy from Libyan soil. It receives illustration from the early elements of Italian religion and some interesting materials for comparison with the Mycenaean pillar shrines are supplied by the sepulchral structures of the Iberic West.

It is possible to point out in some respects a nearer and at the same time a contemporary comparison in the Western Mediterranean area which comes within the ascertained range of Mycenaean intercourse. The great prehistoric buildings of the Maltese islands, commonly but erroneously referred to the Phoenicians, afford unique monumental evidence of a baetylic worship akin to that illustrated by the cult scenes described in the preceding sections.

In the side chapels of the megalithic sanctuaries of Hagiar Kim and the Giganteja aniconic pillar idols are still to be seen either standing in their original place or lying near it. The ground scheme of these great megalithic buildings recalls the internal structure of a chambered barrow with lateral and terminal apse-like cells, but in this case it is by no means certain that the whole was roofed over. The baetylic pillars stood, and in some cases still stand, within the side cells or chapels, at times with an altar block in front of them and shut off originally by separate stone door-ways from the main gallery, the opening of these cells where preserved recalling those of rock tombs such as those of Chaoaach in Tunisia or those of the opposite coastland of south-eastern Sicily. The apse-like walls of the cells form a horizontal vaulting like incomplete bee-hive chambers. At Hagiar Kim a small apse of this kind is worked into the outer wall and within it a baetylic

Fig. 67.—Pillar Cell of Hagiar Kim, Malta.

pillar of a roughly square section with rounded angles stands *in situ*. In front of the pillar is a somewhat hatchet shaped 'altar-stone' decorated with the usual pit markings, and on either side are two large, upright blocks which may have supported a stone lintel forming thus a trilithic portal through which the pillar idol would have appeared much as those within the rustic shrines on the Mycenaean signets. To the right here is a characteristic feature which should not escape notice—a small oval peep-hole or 'squint' giving a view into one of the internal apses of the sanctuary.

In other cases the baetylic column still stands within a dolmen-like cell, of which it helps to support the roof slabs. An example of these cellular shrines is given in Fig. 67.[1] It will be seen that the top of the pillar is surmounted by two slabs, and there is a small interval between

---

[1] From a photograph taken by me in 1897.

them filled with earth, and most probably due to a slight subsidence of the pillar, a subsidence not shared by the upper or roof-slab, the two ends of which rested on the side walls of the chamber. It is further interesting to note that these pillars, the appearance of which through the opening presents such a striking resemblance to those of some of the Mycenaean shrines, have the same characteristic outline tapering towards the base, which has been shown to owe its origin to the necessities of such primitive stone structures. We have here in their typical aspect the 'Pillars of the House,' similar to those of the prehistoric chambered tombs and the primitive monuments of the Balearic Islands,[1] though the shaft in this case is in one piece—a transition to the Mycenaean form.

It is impossible in this place to enter into details as to the character of these Maltese monuments. It must be sufficient here to observe that the view, still widely held, that they were temples built by the Phoenicians,[2] is quite opposed to the archaeological evidence. The Phoenician letters engraved on the rock-floor of the Giganteja might (if they are genuine), give some grounds for supposing that the later Phoenician colonists in the island accepted and adopted a local pillar cult, which in many respects was parallel with their own. But the remains as a whole point to a much more remote period. The bucchero vase fragments, which abound within and around these Maltese monuments,[3] show both in their paste and incised and punctuated decoration a distinct analogy with those of the Second Sikel Period of Orsi, from the opposite coast of Sicily,[4] the date of which is approximately fixed by the imported Mycenaean relics with which they are associated.[5] The window-like openings of the side-cells at Hagiar Kim and Mnaidra have already been compared with those of the Sicilian 'tombe a fenestra,' containing these allied ceramic types. It may be added that the spiral reliefs carved on some of the Sikel door-slabs from the cemetery of Castelluccio, and there recognised as due to Mycenaean influence,[6] find their analogy in the spirally carved blocks of the Giganteja in Gozo. These ornamental blocks form the threshold and side blocks of a lateral apse or chapel which contains a pillar

---

[1] See p. 89.

[2] This view is repeated in Perrot et Chipiez, *L'Art*, &c. iii. p. 306. 'Enfin (ces monuments) nous fournissent des types authentiques sinon élegants et beaux de cette architecture réligieuse des Phéniciens, dont nous savons si peu de chose.'

[3] During a careful exploration of these monuments in 1897 I observed quantities of fragments of this class of pottery in and around the megalithic buildings of Malta and Gozo. A complete bowl of the same kind found at Hagiar Kim with incised scrolls and punctuations, inlaid with chalky matter, is in the Museum at Valletta. Many fragments were simply adorned with punctuations like the decoration of the stones on a small scale; an indication of common origin.

[4] Compare especially some bucchero pottery of this class from the cemetery of Molinello (near Megara Hyblaea) associated in one case with a fragment of imported Mycenaean pottery. P. Orsi, 'Di due Sepolcreti Siculi' (*Arch. Storio Siciliano*, N.S. Anno XVIII.) Tav. iii. and p. 14 *seqq.* One of these vases presents a double point of comparison with the Maltese examples from its combination of the incised linear and punctuated decoration.

[5] Orsi, *Bulletino di Paletnologia Italiana*, 1889, p. 206 Tav. vii. 5, 9: 1891, p. 121; 'Necropoli sicula presso Siracusa con vasi e bronzi Micenei' (*Mon. Antichi*, ii. 1883), &c.

[6] Orsi, 'La Necropoli sicula di Castellucio,' *Bullettino di Paletnologia Italiana*, 1892, pp. 69, 70, Tav. vi.

idol, in this case of conical form. In the section of the Giganteja, drawn for La Marmara,[1] the baetylic cone is still shown in its place within a small dolmen-like cell; at present both the cell and cone are overthrown,[2] though the ornamental blocks in front remain in their places. The two side-blocks which look like altar stones are decorated with a tongue and double volute design, recalling the terminal ornamentation on one of the door-slabs of Castelluccio. The threshold blocks on the other hand are covered with returning spirals with lozenge-shaped interspaces (Fig 68), which point even more clearly than the Sicilian parallels to Aegean models, themselves the derivatives of Egyptian originals. We here in fact

FIG. 68.—SPIRAL ORNAMENT ON THRESHOLD OF BAETYLIC CHAPEL, GIGANTEJA, GOZO.

approach very near the ceiling decoration of Eighteenth and Nineteenth Dynasty tombs.[3]

These sculptured blocks of the Maltese monuments must be reckoned among the later elements contained in them, yet some of them, like the altar with its foliated sides from Hagiar Kim, suggest parallels belonging to the earliest Mycenaean period, as represented by the vegetable motives on a gold cup from the fourth acropolis tomb at Mycenae, and the vases and painted stucco

---

[1] *Nouvelles Annales de l'Institut de Correspondance Archéologique* i. (1832); Perrot et Chipiez, *op. cit.* iii. p. 299, Fig. 222.

The cone is broken in two.

[3] It is possible that the Egyptian influence

here arrived by a Libyan channel, but it is more reasonable to refer it to the same Mycenaean agency that was undoubtedly at work on the opposite Sicilian coast.

fragments of Thera and Therasia.[1] The remarkable steatopygous female images found in the latter building, and absurdly called 'Cabiri,'[2] find a certain parallelism in the adipose marble figures from the prae-Mycenaean sepultures of the Aegean world,[3] but their even more striking conformity with the figures from Naqada[4] belonging to the prehistoric race of Egypt suggest in this case a still older Libyan tradition. The fundamental lines of these megalithic monuments themselves recall the neolithic chambered barrows, with terminal and lateral apses, as found throughout a large Iberic area and, still farther afield, in Britain and the Channel Islands.

We have here then unquestionably *in situ* in the Maltese islands the megalithic sanctuaries of an aniconic cult parallel to that of the Aegean world and of the Semitic lands to the east of it. But the parallel gains additional interest from the fact that we see the actual shrines of this primitive pillar-worship invaded with decorative motives apparently from a Mycenaean source. How far the externals of cult may have been influenced here in other ways from that quarter it is impossible to say. In any case we are brought very near that form of the Mycenaean pillar-worship, the shrines of which have already been compared with the simple dolmen cells still found in India. And what lends especial importance to the parallel is that we see the cone and pillar representatives of spiritual beings associated in the case of these Maltese monuments with structures that stand in a direct funereal relation. In spite of the absence of any adequate archaeological record of the excavations conducted at various times in these monuments there can be no doubt that they served in part at least a sepulchral purpose. The recorded discovery of a human skull in one chamber, the cists still visible in places superimposed on one another, the abundance of pottery, all point to this conclusion. We have here by all seeming the sanctuary of a heroic cult, in which the aniconic image that represented the Departed also marked the place of his last rest.

§ 30.—*An Oriental Pillar Shrine in Macedonia, and the Associated Worship.*

The attachment of the cult of sacred pillars to sepulchral religion as shown by examples from the Greek and Semitic lands, and again by the megalithic structures of the Maltese islands, still asserts itself in the baetylic worship, which has survived to our day under the cloak of Islam throughout the Mohammedan world. It has been already noticed that the mosque at

---

[1] These comparisons were pointed out by me in a paper read at the Ipswich Meeting of the British Association entitled 'Primitive European Idols in the Light of Recent Discoveries,' printed in the *East Anglian Daily Times*, Sept. 19, 1895. Cf. too, *Cretan Pictographs*, &c., p. 129.

[2] Caruana, *Report on the Phoenician, &c. Antiquities from Malta*, pp. 30, 31 and photo-

graph; P. et C., iii. p. 305, Figs. 230, 231.

[3] See *Primitive European Idols*, &c. *loc. cit.* To the steatopygous female figures from Sparta described by Dr. Wolters (*Ath. Mitth.* 1891, p. 52, *seqq.*) may be added an example from Patesia near Athens, now in the Ashmolean Museum.

[4] Petrie, *Nagada and Ballas*, Pl. VI. Figs. 1-4, pp. 13, 14, 34.

Mecca, with its open court and sacred stone, itself preserves the essential features of the primitive Semitic temple. This taking over by the Prophet and his immediate followers of forms derived from the old Arabian stone-worship has singularly favoured the persistence of a kind of Moslem paganism. The Mohammedan lands are strewn with little Caabas, and the turbaned headstones of the 'Saints' Graves,' with which the adoration of such non-sepulchral pillars is closely bound up, must themselves be regarded as the aniconic images of a heroic cult. With changed names and under changed conditions the tomb of Adonis still rises beside the cone of Astarte.

FIG. 69.—SACRED PILLAR IN SHRINE, TEKEKIÖI, MACEDONIA.

But one result of these Mohammedan survivals is that the opportunity still presents itself, in the bye-ways of the East, of actually partaking in the observances of a baetylic ritual, which is in fact the abiding representative of the old Semitic stone-worship. Here and there, even, upon soil that was once Hellenic, the same oriental influence has brought back a local pillar cult essentially the same in character as that which flourished in the Mycenaean world, but which had already, in classical days, receded into the background before the artistic creations of Greek religion. A personal experience may thus supply a more living picture of the actualities of this primitive ritual than can be gained from the discreet references of our biblical sources or the silent evidence of engraved signets and ruined shrines.

In the course of some archaeological investigations in upper Macedonia, I heard of a sacred stone at a Turkish village called Tekekiöi,[1] between Skopia and Istib, which was an object of veneration not only to the native Moslems, but to many Christians from the surrounding regions, who made it an object of pilgrimage on St. George's day. In company with my guide, a Mohammedan Albanian, I visited the spot and found that the stone was contained in a two-roomed shrine under the charge of a Dervish. There was here, in fact, a mosque or 'mesgeda' in the oldest sense of the word, as a shrine of pre-Islamic stone-worship, like that containing the pillar form of the God of Bostra.

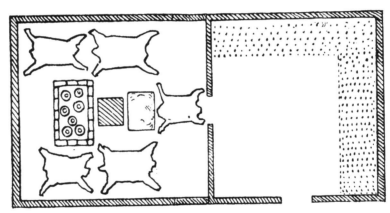

FIG. 70.—PLAN OF SHRINE, TEKEKIÖI, MACEDONIA.

For the better understanding of the ritual employed, I went through the whole ceremony myself. A roomy mud-floored ante-chamber, made for the convenience of the worshippers, communicated by an inner doorway with the shrine of the stone itself. The 'holy of holies' within was a plain square chamber, in the centre of which rose the sacred pillar (Figs. 69, 70). Like the baetylic stones of antiquity, it might be said to have 'fallen from heaven,' for, according to the local legend, it had flown here over a thousand years since from Khorassan.[2] The pillar consisted of an upright stone of square section with bevelled angles about 6½ feet high and 1¼ feet thick, supporting another smaller and somewhat irregular block. Both were black and greasy from secular anointing, recalling the time-honoured practice of

---

[1] The name of the village (= Village of the Teke) in its Slavonic form is Tečino Selo. It lies in the hills a little north of the track from Skopia (Üsküb) to Istib, a short day's

journey from the former place.

[2] According to one account it was brought to its present position by a holy man from Bosnia.

pouring oil on sacred stones as Jacob did at Bethel.[1] On one side of this ' Niger Lapis ' is a kind of sunken hearth-stone, upon which are set candlesticks of antique form for the nightly illumination of the stone—a distant reminiscence of the Phoenician candlestick altars and cressets, such as those seen on either side of the cone at Paphos upon some well-known coin-types. On the other side of the pillar is a small stone base, on which the votary stands for his prayers and ritual observances. The floor is strewn with the fleeces of sacrificed rams, and on the walls are suspended triangular plait-work offerings made of ears of corn, placed here by votaries who desire. to draw forth from the Spirit of the stone a beneficent influence on their crops.

Taking his stand on the flat stone by the pillar, the suppliant utters a prayer for what he most wishes, and afterwards embraces the stone in such a way that the finger tips meet at its further side. A sick Albanian was walking round the pillar when I first saw it, kissing and embracing it at every turn.

The worshipper who would conform to the full ritual, now fills a keg of water from a spring that rises near the shrine—another primitive touch,— and makes his way through a thorny grove up a neighbouring knoll, on which is a wooden enclosure surrounding a Mohammedan Saint's Grave or Tekke.[2] Over the headstone of this grows a thorn-tree hung with rags of divers colours, attached to it—according to a wide-spread primitive rite—by sick persons who had made a pilgrimage to the tomb. The turbaned column itself represents in aniconic shape the visible presence of the departed Saint, and, conjointly with the thorn-bush, a material abode for the departed Spirit, so that we have here a curious illustration of the ancient connexion between Tree and Pillar worship.

In the centre of the grave was a hole, into which the water from the holy spring was poured, and mixed with the holy earth. Of this the votary drinks three times,[3] and he must thrice anoint his forehead with it. This draught is the true Arabian *solwān*, or ' draught of consolation.[4]

It was now necessary to walk three times round the grave, each time kissing and touching with the forehead the stone at the head and foot of it. A handful of the grave dust was next given me, to be made up into a

[1] Gen. xxvii. 18; xxxv. 14. See above, p. 34. Compare Robertson Smith, *Religion of the Semites*, p. 232, who illustrates the late survival of the practice by the ' lapis pertusus ' at Jerusalem described by the pilgrim from Bordeaux in the fourth century of our era. ' Ad quem veniunt Judaei singulis annis et ungunt eum.' Near Sidon the practice of anointing sacred stones with oil—in this case strangely enough Roman milestones—goes on to this day; Pietschmann, *Geschichte der Phönizier*, p. 207. Theophrastus (16), makes the superstitious man anoint and worship smooth stones at the cross-ways. The practice itself is connected with the oriental custom of

anointing living persons as a sign of honour (cf. Psalm xlv. 7) which still survives in the case of kings and ecclesiastical dignitaries.

[2] Near it was a wooden coffer for money offerings.

[3] It is permitted to drink it through a cloth or kerchief.

[4] Robertson Smith, *op. cit.*, p. 322. N. 3 remarks that this draught ' that makes the mourner forget his grief, consists of water with which is mingled dust from the grave (Wellhausen, p. 142), a form of communion precisely similar in principle to the Australian usage of eating a small piece of the corpse.

triangular amulet and worn round the neck. An augury of pebbles, which were shuffled about under the Dervish's palms over a hollowed stone, having turned out propitious,[1] we now proceeded to the sacrifice. This took place outside the sepulchral enclosure, where the Priest of the Stone was presently ready with a young ram.[2] My Albanian guide cut its throat, and I was now instructed to dip my right hand little finger in the blood and to touch my forehead with it.

The sacrifice completed, we made our way down again to the shrine, while peals of thunder rolled through the glen from the Black Mountain above. It was now necessary to divest one's self of an article of clothing for the Dervish to wrap round the sacred pillar, where it remained all night. Due offerings of candles were made, which, as evening drew on, were lit on the sunken hearth beside the stone. We were given three barley corns to eat, and a share in the slaughtered ram, of which the rest was taken by the priest, was set apart for our supper in the adjoining antechamber. Here beneath the same roof with the stone, and within sight of it through the open doorway, we were bidden to pass the night, so that the occult influences due to its spiritual possession might shape our dreams as in the days of the patriarchs.

ARTHUR J. EVANS.

---

[1] The hands were separated, still palms downwards, and the numbers of the pebbles under the right and left hand respectively were then counted.

[2] Near him was a kind of low gallows from which was suspended a three-pointed flesh-hook for hanging up the meat. This flesh-hook had to be touched three times with the tip of the right hand little finger.

FRESCO REPRESENTING FAÇADE OF MYCENAEAN TEMPLE.